Steps of Transformation

STEPS OF

AN ORTHODOX PRIEST

EXPLORES THE

TWELVE STEPS

ARCHIMANDRITE MELETIOS WEBBER

ANCIENT FAITH
PUBLISHING

Chesterton, Indiana

STEPS OF TRANSFORMATION:
An Orthodox Priest Explores the Twelve Steps
Copyright © 2003 by Meletios (Peter H.) Webber

Published by   Ancient Faith Publishing
                A division of Ancient Faith Ministries
                P.O. Box 748
                Chesterton, IN 46304

Printed in the United States of America

ISBN 978-1-888212-63-1

The icon of St. Panteleimon appearing on page 10 and the details from the icon
of the Parable of the Prodigal Son appearing on pages 15 and 101 are by Tatiana
Romanova Grant.

25 24 23 22 21   8 7 6 5 4

Dedication:

For Gene

Contents

Part I: The Problem of Addiction and an Overview of the Twelve Steps

Part 2: The Twelve Steps

I express immense gratitude to:

The Right Reverend Bishop Kallistos (Ware) of Diokleia
Rebecca Henson
Maria Thomas
Gerard Gardiner
Professor Rick Otte
Victoria Joy Hoularis-Buksa
The Very Rev. Michael Rymer
Elizabeth Tomlinson
The Rev. Dr. John Chryssavgis
The Very Rev. Thomas Hopko
Dr. David and Christine Delvin
The Very Rev. David Barr
The Rev. C. Paul Schroeder
Mari and Tonni Kuchler
Susan and Simon Fisher
Tatiana Romanova Grant
Deborah Franck
Anastasia Delvecchio
Susan and Alan Webber
Jean and Douglas Webber
the members of the parish of Prophet Elias Greek
    Orthodox Church in Santa Cruz, California
and most especially the very many men and women of
    Alcoholics Anonymous who have helped me form
    the ideas and impressions contained in this book.

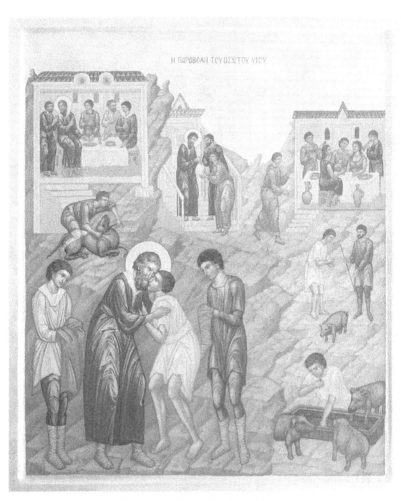

Parable of the Prodigal Son
icon by Tatiana Romanova Grant

Foreword

I AM INDEED GRATEFUL to be given the opportunity to commend
the present book by Fr. Meletios, my valued friend for more than
thirty years. It has taught me many things about the Fellowship of
Alcoholics Anonymous—with which I have never been personally
in contact—and many things also about myself. To the best of my
knowledge, it is the first time that a book of this kind has been
written by an Orthodox priest.

Fr. Meletios provides a convincing answer to a question that
is frequently raised. Can an Orthodox Christian, it is asked, while
still remaining fully loyal to the Church, at the same time turn for
help to AA? Should we not rather put our trust in the Sacraments
of Confession, Anointing (*Evchelaion*), and Holy Communion, and
in the counsel and prayers of our spiritual father? Why seek help
elsewhere? Does this signify a lack of faith?

To this Fr. Meletios replies—and I agree with him—that membership in AA in no way contradicts or undermines membership in
the Church. Quite simply, the two are not rivals, not in competition;
for AA makes no claim to be a church or a religion. The Twelve Steps,
as Fr. Meletios emphasizes, "will never replace the Gospels as the call
of Christ." The meetings of AA are not in any sense a substitute for
participation in the sacramental worship of the Church.

Membership in AA will not make us less Orthodox, or less
Catholic, or less whatever else we are. What AA can do—what,
indeed, it has actually done for innumerable believing Christians—is
to enable them to live out their faith and to experience the power
of the Sacraments in a way that they had not otherwise found
possible. For again and again this has been the experience of the
many thousands, if not millions, who have turned to AA : *it works*.
Its distinctive blend of spirituality and practicality has proved
remarkably successful in the contemporary world. But the rules of
AA, while simple, are certainly not easy.

Fr. Meletios draws attention to various points of contact between AA and the Orthodox tradition. I myself noticed three things in particular that AA shares with a book to which I have devoted many thousands of hours as translator, *The Philokalia*. Both are saying to us, each in its own way:

1. *Live in the present moment:* "See, *now* is the acceptable time; see, *now* is the day of salvation" (2 Corinthians 6:2). We can only make decisions in the present moment, and we can only encounter God in the present moment. As the members of AA insist, "One day at a time."

2. *No one is saved alone:* "We are members of one another" (Ephesians 4:25). Where *The Philokalia* speaks more of spiritual fatherhood and motherhood, the Fellowship of AA is based upon spiritual brotherhood and sisterhood. But the underlying principle is the same: in the words of Fr. Meletios, "Action requires interaction." We are healed by sharing our experience with each other, by listening to each other.

3. *We depend upon a Power greater than ourselves:* "Without Me you can do nothing" (John 15:5). There are few if any of Christ's sayings that *The Philokalia* quotes more often than this. In every human situation we are going to say to ourselves, in the words of Fr. Meletios, "I cannot, God can, and I am going to let Him." In common with Orthodox theology, AA thinks in terms of *synergeia,* of the creative cooperation between divine grace and human freedom. What God does is immeasurably greater than what we do, but the active involvement of our free will is also essential. For, as Fr. Meletios reminds us, repentance (like forgiveness) is not a feeling but a decision.

Here is a book that will help many who, so far as they know, are not themselves alcoholics; for there are numerous kinds of addiction besides the addiction to alcohol, and who among us can claim to be totally free from all addictive weakness? This is a humble and realistic book, full of hope, that bears witness to the immense patience and mercy of God. Let us read it in a spirit of humility and self-questioning, and it will speak to our hearts and to our will.

+ Bishop KALLISTOS of Diokleia

Holy Monastery of St John the Theologian,
Patmos

St Panteleimon

The Church is a hospital, the Sacraments are the medicine, and the Saints who participate in the life of Christ are the doctors. St. Panteleimon, a notable healing saint, has been instrumental in the healing of countless men and women through the centuries.

Holy Passion-bearer and healer Panteleimon,
Intercede with the Merciful God
That He may grant forgiveness to our souls.

Introduction

The Twelve Steps and Their Use

THIS BOOK HAS TWO MAIN PURPOSES: The first is to explore the Twelve Steps of the Fellowship of Alcoholics Anonymous, to explain them to those who may be unfamiliar with them, and to show why the Steps are important in helping people recover from alcoholism (and from other addictive conditions).

The second purpose of this book is to present the Twelve Steps in such a way that members of the Orthodox Church might find them a valuable resource for their own personal spiritual development, should they choose to use them. Furthermore, even though most of the issues discussed will be illustrated using examples from the life of the Orthodox Church, it is hoped that members of other Christian traditions may also find this material helpful as they continue on their spiritual journey.

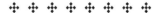

THERE ARE MANY PEOPLE who know (or know of) someone who is a member of Alcoholics Anonymous or one of the many other groups ("Fellowships") that use the Twelve Steps of Alcoholics Anonymous[1] as a basis for their plan of recovery. In watching the recovering person's struggles and successes, an onlooker may have many questions about what is happening and what that person is actually trying to do. Moreover, many people may have heard of the Twelve Steps and yet be quite vague as to their contents, in much the same way that people pay lip service to the Ten Commandments without actually being sure what the Ten Commandments are.

---

1 The original text of the Twelve Steps can be found on pp. 19–20. A slightly modified form of the Steps, which can be used in all circumstances, is to be found in Appendix A, p.205.

This book attempts to explain this process of recovery from addiction in terms which should be familiar to members of the Orthodox Church and members of other religious traditions. Further, this book is also intended as a source book for clergy, for people in the caring professions, and for other interested friends and relatives who might want to know what the Twelve Steps are all about, without actually committing themselves to one or more of the groups who practice them.

There is a strong opinion, held by experts in many fields,[2] that persons who are doing the Twelve Steps because they are addicted to a particular substance or a particular behavior are engaged in the one activity that will give them the best hope of recovery. Such people benefit from being surrounded by others who, at the very least, understand why they are doing what they are doing.

Alcoholics are addicted to alcohol, and their condition is generally obvious to those who know them. Others are addicted to other substances, and still others are addicted to dangerous or antisocial behaviors. Although some addictions are very difficult to detect, each is potentially as devastating as alcoholism in its most virulent form.

Addiction, whether to a substance or to a behavior, is such a common phenomenon in the modern world that it is often necessary to deal with it before other, more traditional, forms of spiritual education can be attempted. Just as people suffering from a manic-depressive disorder need to have their mood swings stabilized before they can effectively use other forms of treatment, so addicts need to address their addictions before they can profitably use other traditional means of spiritual growth. In fact, using traditional methods of spiritual encouragement with addicts and alcoholics is usually fruitless, and may actually do more harm than good.

It is possible that everyone alive, particularly anyone who lives in relative affluence, is affected by addiction in one form or another. In theory, at the very least, it may be very beneficial for as many

---

2 A large amount of material related to statistics and alcohol can be obtained from the National Council on Alcoholism and Drug Dependence (website: http//:www.ncadd.org).

people as possible to have at least some knowledge of the Twelve Steps and how they work.

Until comparatively recently, the Orthodox Church was at home in, and largely confined to, Greece, the Middle East, and beyond. The Twelve Steps are the result of an American spiritual culture, and a Protestant one at that. Nevertheless, on close examination the two traditions can be seen to share a great deal in common. Since the Church and the Fellowship of Alcoholics Anonymous (AA) are not in competition with each other in any sense, it is my hope that in reading about AA's plan of recovery, the reader may not only find out more about this important aspect of modern life, but may also come to a deeper understanding of his or her own religious tradition. It is possible that even a brief glance at the Steps may be enough to encourage a person to live the Orthodox faith with greater awareness and clarity.

Furthermore, since each of the Twelve Steps can be shown to share some element in the thought and experience, the Scripture and prayer life, of the Orthodox Church, I hope to demonstrate that it is quite possible for Orthodox Christians to incorporate these Steps into their own lives in order to deepen their spiritual experience.

For the purposes of the present work, the themes of the Twelve Steps are used in relative isolation from the history of their development.[3] Those wishing to learn more of the thinking behind the Steps are directed to the two major commentaries written by their author. One is in chapters 5, 6, and 7 of *Alcoholics Anonymous* (nicknamed "the Big Book" since the early days of the Fellowship) and the other in the first half of the book *Twelve Steps and Twelve Traditions* (often called the "Twelve and Twelve"). Both were written by one of the cofounders of Alcoholics Anonymous, known to the Fellowship as Bill W.

If anyone reading this book thinks that he may be an alcoholic,

---

3 For a thorough and balanced account of the history of Alcoholics Anonymous, see *A.A. The Story* by Ernest Kurtz, Harper/Hazelden, 1988. This book had been published earlier with the intriguing title *Not-God: A History of Alcoholics Anonymous*.

or even fears that he might be, his best hope for recovery would be to put down this book and get in contact with a local group of AA as quickly as possible. An alcoholic needs the Twelve Steps, but he[4] needs them *within* the context of the Fellowship of AA. Very few people manage to achieve sobriety simply by reading about alcoholism and the Steps. Recovery involves action, and action requires interaction with others. Intellectual knowledge alone makes for a poor recovery, at best.

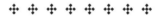

HAVING BECOME PIVOTAL IN THE RECOVERY of hundreds of thousands of alcoholics, the Steps were slowly adapted for use by other groups of people who were engaged in combating addictions other than alcoholism (e.g. Narcotics Anonymous or Cocaine Anonymous), codependency (Al-Anon or Alateen), destructive behaviors (Gamblers Anonymous or Overeaters Anonymous), or destructive imbalances in human behavior (Sex Addicts Anonymous and others). In time, almost all of these Fellowships, each completely independent of all the others, wrote their own "Big Book" (and some also their own "Twelve and Twelve"), describing the experience of the members of that particular Fellowship in using the Twelve Steps as a spiritual weapon in their own lives and in whatever difficulties they found themselves.

Since the Twelve Steps have been successfully adapted for use in situations other than alcoholism, there is an important possibility that they may have a yet more general use, and that they can indeed be used by anyone who needs a boost to his or her spiritual life.

In this book, each Step will be examined in detail, and compared with stories and themes in the Gospels and other parts of Holy Scripture. There will be selections, too, from the prayer life of the Orthodox Church, showing how each of the Steps is reflected in Orthodox life.

---

4 In general, I have opted to use the male pronoun for the drinking alcoholic, simply as a convenience.

Part I

The Problem of Addiction and an Overview of the Twelve Steps

"The younger son gathered all together, journeyed to a far country, and there wasted his possessions with prodigal living. But when he had spent all, there arose a severe famine in that land and he began to be in want. Then he went and joined himself to a citizen of that country, and he sent him into his fields to feed swine. And he would gladly have filled his stomach with the pods that the swine ate, and no one gave him anything." —Luke 15:13–16

Chapter 1

Introduction
to the Twelve Steps

IN THE SECOND HALF OF THE 1930S, a small group of alcoholics got together to confront a problem no one else had managed to solve: how to get rid of their own alcoholism. After a few false starts, they started to get better, or (as they put it) "to recover." They found that by adopting a particular program of action, they were able to stop the downward spiral of their lives and to live, on a daily basis, without the need to drink alcohol.

The Twelve Steps were subsequently written down in order to describe the process by which these people managed to free themselves from the scourge with which they had lived for so long. This experiment, in which alcoholics confronted their own condition and took responsibility for their own recovery, turned out to have unprecedented success. It followed on centuries of other attempts, largely fruitless and futile, in which the general aim was to get rid of alcoholism in other people.

From the point of view of an alcoholic coming into AA, it is hardly important how the Steps came to be written or what philosophical frame of mind brought them into existence. What is important to such a person (or indeed, anyone considering using the Steps) is that, so far as addiction is concerned, the Steps outline a method of recovery which has been shown to be more successful than almost all other forms of treatment put together.

Although they were not aware of it at the time, the actions of these first members of AA were to cause a major shift in society's thinking regarding the nature of addiction in general and of alcoholism in particular. The founders of AA and their closest friends began to talk and write about how they were recovering from alcoholism and about their understanding of alcoholism as a life-threatening, physical disease. The thinking of these first members of AA was in stark contrast with what had been taken for granted during most of human history, that alcoholism was a *moral* weakness, or simply *a sin*. In the years that followed, the medical profession largely came to agree with AA about the nature of the condition. Alcoholism is a physical disease, in that it has definable physical characteristics, a cause, a progression, and a treatment. It slowly became possible to view alcoholism as something susceptible to treatment, no longer to be written off as a criminal condition or a mere weakness of human folly.

However—and this is the great surprise—the treatment for this medical condition turns out to be something quite different from the normal, medical model. Pharmaceutical prescriptions, surgery, and other procedures play little or no part in the treatment of alcoholism. Obviously, too, the condition has implications for mental health, and if treated, both medical and mental health improve.

But that is still not the whole picture, since the traditional methods of mental health treatment do not work either.

The greatest surprise is that the most successful treatment for this physical and mental disease turns out to be *spiritual* in nature. This word "spiritual" is a difficult word to pin down. It is easier to recognize and to experience than to define, but it generally means something to do with one's connectedness with God and with the rest of the universe. This concept will be examined more closely in Chapter 5.

There is another dimension to this issue which must be confronted, even though to do so is hardly comfortable for those who profess to be religious. It seems fairly clear that if this "spiritual" treatment becomes too religious, the healing stops. Put more succinctly, if this spiritual treatment becomes too religious, it hardly gets a chance to start. To be successful, the treatment has to be based on a spirituality that stops short of blossoming into a religious faith. It has to be a spirituality in which God Himself remains anonymous.

Although initially frustrating to anyone with a strong religious faith, this apparent weakness turns out to be the source of the greatest strength in the program of recovery. Indeed, it also provides a very sound basis for subsequent religious faith. There are very important reasons why this strange phenomenon should be as it is, and it is the underlying intention of this book to describe not only why it has to be like that, but also how this phenomenon can be used to strengthen and develop a person's spirituality within his or her own religious tradition.

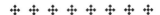

THE STORY OF THE FIRST MEMBERS OF AA is so intriguing that it deserves closer attention. It all started in the mid-1930s when two men, a doctor and a stockbroker, both seriously ill, started to get better from the condition of alcoholism that was destroying them. Having been abandoned to their fate by the medical profession, and tolerated at best by those who loved them most, these men adopted a course of action which not only allowed them to stop drinking (one day at a time), but also allowed them to grow spiritually, and to regain something of the dignity and purpose of life of which their illness had robbed them.

One of the men, known in the world of recovery as "Bill W.," wrote down the basic pattern of what they had done. Actually, by the time he wrote the story down, the two men had been joined in recovery by a good number of others, both men and women, all of whom had, at one time or another, been written off by the rest of the world as hopeless alcoholics.

In examining what Bill W. wrote, there are some surprises. Anyone who expects to find a list of ways to stop drinking is going to be very disappointed. This is how the program appears in "How It Works," Chapter 5 of *Alcoholics Anonymous*.

> Here are the steps we took, which are a suggested program of recovery:
> 1. We admitted we were powerless over alcohol—that our lives had become unmanageable.
> 2. Came to believe that a power greater than ourselves could restore us to sanity.

3. Made a decision to turn our will and our lives over to the care of God *as we understood Him.*
4. Made a searching and fearless moral inventory of ourselves.
5. Admitted to God, to ourselves, and to another human being the exact nature of our wrongs.
6. Were entirely ready to have God remove all these defects of character.
7. Humbly asked Him to remove our shortcomings.
8. Made a list of all persons we had harmed, and became willing to make amends to them all.
9. Made direct amends to such people wherever possible, except when to do so would injure them or others.
10. Continued to take personal inventory and when we were wrong promptly admitted it.
11. Sought through prayer and meditation to improve our conscious contact with God *as we understood Him,* praying only for knowledge of His will for us and the power to carry that out.
12. Having had a spiritual awakening as the result of these steps, we tried to carry this message to alcoholics, and to practice these principles in all our affairs.[5]

What is immediately noticeable is that the Steps hardly mention alcohol, and they say nothing obvious about how to stop drinking. They mention nothing about going to meetings or getting a

---

5 The Twelve Steps and Twelve Traditions are reprinted with permission of Alcoholics Anonymous World Services, Inc. (AAWS). Permission to reprint the Twelve Steps and Twelve Traditions does not mean that AAWS has reviewed or approved the contents of this publication, or that AA necessarily agrees with the views expressed herein. AA is a program of recovery from alcoholism *only*—use of the Twelve Steps and Twelve Traditions in connection with programs and activities which are patterned after AA, but which address other problems, or in any other non-AA context, does not imply otherwise. Additionally, while AA is a spiritual program, AA is not a religious program. Thus, AA is not affiliated or allied with any sect, denomination, or specific religious belief.

sponsor, nothing about staying away from bars and parties; they make no threats and offer no advice. They do not say, "1. Stop drinking. 2. Go to AA meetings. 3. Keep busy, but don't get tired," and so on. In fact, apart from the word "alcohol" in the First Step and the word "alcoholics" in the Twelfth Step, they do not even mention the problem.

What the Steps do is simply to list a number of actions which some people took, and these actions are entirely spiritual in nature.

Certainly this was a novel approach to the problem, quite unlike most things that had been tried in the past. It seemed to work—at least some of the time—and that was better than anything else that had been tried before.

The group that grew up around the two original men (Bill W. and Dr. Bob) has now grown in size to a Fellowship of several million members who live in almost every country in the world. AA literature has been translated into a large number of languages and made available to people who need it. Most recently, there has been considerable need to provide the experience, strength, and hope of AA in countries of the former Soviet Union.

Even though the Steps originated in the experience of those dying from alcoholism, almost at once they were adapted for use by the families (most often the wives) and friends of those alcoholics. The purpose of this adaptation was to encourage the families and friends of alcoholics to work on their own spiritual development and not (as most would expect) to get the alcoholic to stop drinking. Al-Anon and Alateen are still very active fellowships, for the relatives and friends, and the children of alcoholics respectively. Each Fellowship has its own parallel organization, kept separate from the organization of AA.

Later still, the Twelve Steps were adapted for use by large numbers of others who discovered that the pattern of action they contained provided an opportunity for recovery from a wide variety of addictions and compulsions, each of which was capable of making life difficult, if not impossible. Fellowships that focus on gambling, sex addiction, food-related problems, and recovery from incest and other traumatic events have all profitably used the Twelve Steps to encourage their members to discover and follow a path to spiritual recovery.

In this book, it is the life and experience of Alcoholics Anonymous that will most often be used as an example to explain the significance of each of the Steps. Alcoholism has a particular status as the "elder brother" in the world of addiction. However, almost everything said in the context of alcoholism can be transferred, with little effort, to other addictions and behaviors, and then—through a more general application—go on to provide insight for all men and women of good will.

THE FELLOWSHIP OF ALCOHOLICS ANONYMOUS is not a church. It has no religious teachings, no scriptures, no saints, and no priesthood. It has no initiation, no services, no sacraments, and no feast days. It does not offer its members salvation, it is unconcerned with an afterlife, and it confers no blessings. What AA offers is sobriety, and it does so to anyone who has a desire to stop drinking.

Nevertheless, the Fellowship of AA and the Twelve Steps that lie at the heart of its life have a definite religious ring about them. God is mentioned often during meetings and extensively in the literature. The Steps themselves talk of forgiveness, of shortcomings, and of making amends. They even talk of prayer and meditation. Even so, AA points out that these activities are not "religious" but "spiritual." The AA path is spiritual and open to all who need it. For religion, the members of the Fellowship must look elsewhere, and in practice they are actively encouraged to do just that. AA places absolutely no limits on the influence any given religion might have on individual members, so long as it does not conflict with the sole requirement for AA membership: the "desire to stop drinking." How this principle is worked out in the practice of the alcoholic's religion is left entirely to the individual to define.

It will be necessary, then, to describe exactly how AA defines the terms "religious" and "spiritual." A difference in meaning has to be established in order to arrive at a deeper understanding of the issue, not least because most religious people use the two words to mean more or less the same thing. The two terms grew apart in the experience of the members of AA as they began to give vocabulary to the process of recovery. It is crucial that people of strong religious traditions (including the Orthodox) come to terms with this distinction if they are going to find the help they need when they turn to the Steps.

The genius of the political system of the United States lies in the separation of Church and State, since it leaves each free to continue its work with little chance that the Church's eternal mission and absolute values will be compromised by the needs of government. In a similar way, the distinction between "religious" and "spiritual" is the genius of AA. It allows men and women of all religions or none to gather together before God (as each person understands "God") in order to find a solution to a life-threatening disease, and it does so without challenging or changing the religious beliefs of anyone.

To some religious people, including members of the Orthodox Church, this may present a threat to their own sense of security. If anyone has feelings of spiritual superiority (not, unfortunately, an uncommon phenomenon), those feelings will be challenged too. However, the results of this challenge may also turn out to be beneficial. Often when a sense of religious conviction is held in a spirit of humility and gratitude, that conviction is strengthened, not diminished.

It is important to point out that there is no such thing as Orthodox AA, any more than there is Catholic AA, or Protestant AA, or Jewish AA. The focus of AA is alcoholism, not religion. Indeed, from the earliest history of the Fellowship there have been examples of people of different religious traditions working together within the Fellowship, even during periods when most religious groups regarded every other religious group with a great deal of suspicion, if not with downright hostility. There is an exceptionally strong sense of identity in AA. Every member is a brother or sister to every other member at a level most egalitarian political philosophies can only dream of. There tends to be an easy, trusting intimacy among its members, even when two people meet for the first time. In fact, two people who have been to the gates of hell and back have a great deal more in common with each other than the ties that nationhood or religious affiliation can supply. Two people striving to uncover the same recovery find immediate identity in each other, even if those two people go in completely different directions when it comes to an expression of their religious life. That they can do so without causing any rift in their relationship is simply part of the miracle.

According to the way AA is organized, it *is* possible for the membership of a particular church to maintain its own AA group, so long as the group is not officially affiliated with that church, and so long as the group is open to any who might want to stop drinking. In practice, however, it is often found that the main focus of AA ("the desire to stop drinking") makes such groupings unnecessary. In general, AA groups are made stronger by having a wide range of experience, including religious experience. In cases where religious AA groups have been established, or where people have gone on to form their own Fellowships based on an exclusive religious viewpoint, such groups tend to remain small and isolated, and even though they may be highly vocal, their influence is not widespread compared with the outreach of AA as a whole.

It is sometimes said that the genius of America is practicality, and that the people of America are very good at taking a theory and making it work in practice. This is true when applied to the development of political liberty in the eighteenth century. It may be equally true in the development of recovery from addiction in the twentieth century. The Steps are a collection of straightforward, common-sense, age-old ideas, gathered from a number of sources. They take practical, obvious measures to achieve a goal, one Step at a time. Trying to achieve them all at once is normally beyond the scope of any one human being. Put in a sensible order, they are quite capable of being accomplished one at a time.

The distinct blend of spirituality and practicality is one of the most outstanding elements of the overall beauty and attraction of the Twelve Steps, and constitutes the major reason for their being such an important contribution to the life of the twentieth century and beyond.

The Problem

Addiction is a terrible and mysterious thing. It is life-destroying, and even worse, it is soul-destroying. It destroys people from the inside out, devastates families, and, in general, provides the world with a model of dysfunction, with attributes that most people can recognize from their own experience of life.

The Twelve Steps came from the experience of alcoholics, and for this reason it is sometimes helpful to examine the mind of the alcoholic in order to see why a particular idea is represented in the Steps. This will be the main focus in Chapter 2. Naturally, not everyone will need to admit having alcoholic characteristics, but it might be helpful to consider those characteristics in order to grasp the deeper significance of a particular Step and to apply that knowledge to one's own situation.

Fortunately, almost everything that can be said to be true for alcoholism is true also for other forms of dysfunctional behavior in general and addictive behavior in particular. Many people, at some stage in their lives, get into trouble with one of the four major areas of difficulty: money, food, addictive drugs, and sex, with time and personal power providing fifth and sixth dimensions. Put in a way that is perhaps more hopeful, many human beings tend to get into trouble, at some time in their lives, with the way they interact with the rest of the world, and the misuse of time, power, food, sex, addictive substances, or money is generally the symptom of that difficulty.

All addictions are dangerous, and all can be fatal. They represent a deep and lasting disturbance within the human personality. Most addicts long to be rid of their addiction, but seem to be able to do nothing to break themselves free. In general, drinking alcoholics want to get better, and certainly want freedom from the pain and the chaos in their lives. Unfortunately, they also do not want to have to do anything to achieve that goal, and they often believe there is absolutely nothing they can do to help themselves.

For the drinking alcoholic, almost every method of avoiding the effects of alcoholism will have been tried at one time or another, and most will have failed. Prayer (with or without solemn oaths) will, in most cases, have proved ineffectual. Some people have entered monasteries to try to find the answer; others have joined the Foreign Legion. Moving house, moving city, or even moving country never seems to work. Imprisonment sometimes works, but only for the period of actual incarceration, and sometimes not even then. A number of years ago, I used to visit a young man in a locked ward in a large teaching hospital in London. He was being treated for heroin addiction, and was also being held in custody. For all the show of security and surveillance, I discovered that his daily supply of heroin was limited only by his ability to pay for it, and that throughout his time there he continued to run a lucrative dealership in heroin from the hospital bed in which he was soon to die.

If an alcoholic is put in prison, or in the middle of Saudi Arabia (officially an alcohol-free country), has his hands tied behind his back and all his money taken away—he will still generally find a way of getting hold of the drug for which his body craves. Even in an alcohol-soaked mind, there is no limit to the amount of effort the addict can make in obtaining his drug. At a level that transcends the conscious and subconscious mind, the addict believes he needs alcohol more than anything else in the world. Yet his devotion is flawed and desperate. He loves his drug and hates his drug in equal measures. He loves himself and hates himself with the same intensity.

If addiction were any less baffling, it would not be addiction. Addiction is not logical, and so it cannot respond to reason. It is a circular, downward-spiraling process which ensures that the person who is hooked always gets worse, never better. It places the desired "high" just out of his reach, necessitating deeper involvement, more risk, more danger, more shame, and more guilt. Occasionally, the addiction can be put on hold for months or even years, only to take over again at a moment's notice when a suitable place and time are reached.

The Solution

The Twelve Steps of Alcoholics Anonymous are the best solution to addiction found so far. Most of the solutions that the alcoholic may have tried before would have involved attempts to change everybody else in the world. Indeed, to a drinking alcoholic, attempting to change the rest of the world seems like a sensible thing to do. However, when he stands at the foot of the Steps, the alcoholic is suddenly and painfully confronted with the awareness that *he needs to change himself.*

Changing oneself is not something that human beings find easy, and in general there has to be strong motivation to achieve it. Unfortunately, the best and most successful motivation for making such a change and starting the Twelve Steps is fear of death—or something very similar. Anything less tends to produce less than the needed results. However, once a person comes face-to-face with death (whether real or imagined), his outlook often (but not always) alters to the extent that he will start making changes which he would not or could not contemplate before.

This, in the parlance of AA, is what is meant by "hitting bottom." It is at once the most fruitful and the most painful of human conditions. Having hit bottom, the individual is aware that unless he does something drastic, there is either no future at all, or a very bleak one. For alcoholics, "bottom" happens when the future promises nothing but death, perhaps with the threat of imprisonment or insanity thrown in. For those with other addictions, the future is no brighter, although the actual details of the hopeless future may vary. The gambler who has spent his children's future, or the sex addict who has just infected his spouse with the AIDS virus, knows a level of misery which is, happily, unknown to the rest of the world. However, the deep tragedy of events like this proves to be a good starting point for recovery. They "bring the person to himself" (just like the prodigal son), and allow the process of recovery and repentance to begin.

No one in his right mind would do the Twelve Steps unless there were very good reasons for doing so. The Steps look risky and dangerous, because they seem to invite a person to put himself at a disadvantage; they make him admit his weakness and acknowledge his need for help. The Steps invite honesty, and a close examination of things that are not right in the life of the addict. No alcoholic in his right (addicted) mind wants to do anything like that.

This is what often separates people doing the Twelve Steps from people who are deeply involved with the religious life. At most levels, religious activity has to do with the *quality* of life. Doing the Twelve Steps has more to do with the *quantity* of life, and the individual (in the first case, the alcoholic) is aware that if he does not do the Steps with some seriousness, he is in danger of drinking again. Drinking again will lead, ultimately, to death, and a painful, shameful death at that. The sort of effort needed to make the Twelve Steps work is usually only matched by people who live in the strictest of monasteries, or those in the specialized teams of the armed services. Outside monasteries and the armed forces, seldom is a person asked to do anything with such vigor.

If the recovering alcoholic can attain, and live with, a level of spirituality, he will live. If he cannot, he will die.

The *physical* life of an addict depends on his *spiritual* life.

A surprising element, in the light of what has just been said, is that the Twelve Steps have their fullest meaning and significance in a situation where a person has no spiritual qualification, and where ordination, university degrees, and social standing are of absolutely no importance. Professional people, including doctors and priests and even politicians, who attempt to do the Twelve Steps for any reason generally have to start by refinding the "self" within themselves. The Twelve Steps cannot be done easily by someone who is primarily aware of his or her own status, or who thinks of him- or herself as being in any way special. It is the feeling of being special that tends to get alcoholics into trouble in the first place. This phenomenon is sometimes called "terminal uniqueness"—it is a method of thinking which allows the alcoholic to feel that he can justify living the alcoholic lifestyle: "Who wouldn't drink, if they had my problems?" Addiction is much easier if one believes that one is a special case . . . special all the way to the cemetery.

Thinking of oneself as a special case, or making oneself into the victim of circumstances, is an important part of the process of coping with life as a drinking alcoholic. Both being special and being a victim will need to be put aside if a person is to find a lasting and meaningful recovery.

In the reality of a drinking alcoholic, life is a terrifying and confusing game in which his aim is to go on as long as possible without allowing himself to be fenced in by circumstances. It is a balancing act, full of pitfalls and booby traps. Unfortunately, the alcoholic can only continue in this condition if he is forever imposing his diseased sense of self-preservation on those around him. In time, it becomes obvious (though not necessarily palatable) to everyone around him that the most important relationship in the life of the addict is the relationship with his drug; everything else is subsidiary to it, and has to be twisted, bent, or forced to fall into line with that reality.

Although he does not realize it, the moment the alcoholic starts to create his own reality, and subsequently manages to manipulate anyone and everyone to enter into that reality, he is in deep spiritual danger. The danger exists because creating reality is essentially the work of God. What the alcoholic is actually trying to do is to *be* God.

In many senses, the alcoholic believes that his own diseased will has to be "god," since anything else would force him to accept the *real* reality which the real God has created, and that would force him to give up the most precious thing he has—his relationship with his drug.

Although the most noticeable symptoms of alcoholism are almost entirely physiological, the inner core of the disease is different: it is a defect in the human will. Conversely, recovery from alcoholism means the restoration of the human will, as God first intended. Only after that has happened is the person able to start using the age-old methods and techniques of spiritual development.

The Steps do not require any religious knowledge or training on the part of the individual, neither do they require that person to belong to any church. The Steps were written to encourage newcomers to AA to start on a program of recovery. Had they demanded that newcomers subscribe to a particular religious faith, most of those people would have left immediately. It is worth bearing in mind that drinking alcoholics, by their very nature, are very suspicious, because from their point of view the whole world seems to be full of people who are intent on making them do things that they do not want to do. They trust no one; they often have very grave reservations about their own religious tradition (if they have one), and certainly have absolutely no time for the religious tradition of anyone else. On the other hand, the average alcoholic on entering AA knows very well how to pray, even if he does not believe in God. Time and time again he will have asked God to help him stop drinking, but since God has (up to this very point) not seen fit to do such a thing unless the alcoholic starts taking responsibility for his own actions (which, by virtue of his condition, he absolutely cannot do), he has likely decided that God is either deaf or dead. Actually, drinking alcoholics also tend to love theology, as well as any other speculative thinking which allows them to hold strong opinions without having to justify them in any way. However, no theology is presented to them in AA, so they can have nothing to struggle with. They are presented instead with God—not the idea of God, but the action of God—and that is very difficult to argue with.

The wording of the Steps does not contain any negative language at all. What is more, they describe a situation that has already taken place. This is for a very good reason. Alcoholics respond very badly to people telling them what to do. If the First Step were phrased: "What you need to do is to see that you are powerless over alcohol, that your life has become unmanageable," it is likely that the alcoholic would spend the rest of his (probably short) life trying to prove the Step wrong.

It is tempting to suppose that alcohol is king in the world of the individual alcoholic, but this is only partly true. It is more accurate to say that it is the ego of the alcoholic, the broken, impaired ego, which is not only his king, but also his god.

This is why it is so important that at the very beginning of his recovery the alcoholic come to terms with the fact that there is a power outside himself which is greater than he is. Something, even in conceptual form, has to displace the broken ego which is playing god. At the beginning it matters little what. As recovery develops in the individual, it may be appropriate too for the idea of a Higher Power to become more and more closely identified with the Supreme Being of the universe, and indeed, as one enters the miraculous realms of recovery, the individual is more and more likely to want to make that connection. At the beginning, however, it is as well to strip down the idea of God, since otherwise all sorts of dangerous notions might be incorporated into the concept, and if that concept then grows roots, it might not be capable of sustaining long-term sobriety. God can only be God if He is completely free of the alcoholic's ego.

It is in the nature of the Twelve Steps that there is no such thing as perfection with regard to doing them. Certainly if someone is using the Steps to recover from alcoholism, many people will assume that the Steps are working properly if that person starts to show signs of recovery, and achieves some level of sobriety. However, the real truth of the success of the Steps lies deep within the heart of the person doing them, and that information is available to God alone.

Concluding Thoughts

There are hundreds of thousands of people throughout the world who, if asked, would state that they owe their entire lives to the Twelve Steps of AA. They do not proclaim the fact in a way which is too obvious, however, since these same people have learned a very healthy and realistic respect for anonymity; they tend not to proclaim their identities openly to the general public. On the other hand, family members and friends are almost certain to know and share with them the sense of joy and relief they now experience.

Recovering alcoholics generally acknowledge that they have been to the gates of hell, but have been dragged back from that place by twelve simple Steps. In looking back, most, if not all, will be able to remember occasions in their lives when they believed that there was no power on earth or in heaven that could relieve them of their alcoholism, and consequently that their inevitable end was imprisonment, insanity, or death. The only question was: When?

Alcoholics in recovery and other recovering addicts have all experienced the possibility of living sober lives, and far from becoming deathly dull, they have found that they have a zest for living which few who have not walked their path can grasp. Nothing makes life look more attractive than the intimate confrontation with death that each one of these people has experienced.

Chapter 2

The Drinking Alcoholic—
Icon of Broken Humanity

A YOUNG MAN WAS ONCE LOST SOMEWHERE in the English country-side. He wandered around for a while, but all the fields looked alike, all the roads seemed unlikely, and he was getting very tired. He wanted to rest, he wanted to clean himself up, and he wanted to have something to eat. Eventually he came across a scruffy old man, obviously a native of the area, leaning over a five-bar gate, chewing on a piece of straw. Our young friend asked the old man how he could get to his particular destination. The old man was thoughtful for a moment, was silent for a while, then looked at him and said, "Ah . . . you can't get there from 'ere."

The impossibility of such a situation does nothing to soften the sense of bewilderment it invokes. It is that bewilderment that sums up the predicament of the drinking alcoholic. He is so stuck in his own difficulties that he can see no possible rescue from his torment. Like a man struggling in quicksand, the more he struggles and attempts to get himself out—in fact, the more he tries to do anything at all—the worse the situation gets, and the deeper he sinks.

The drinking alcoholic is not a worse sinner than anyone else; he just looks as if he is. In fact, once the notion has been accepted that alcoholism is actually a disease and not a moral weakness, it may turn out that there is less sinfulness involved in the life of the alcoholic than might otherwise appear. Yet broken he certainly is, and he is heading for certain ruin. He will never get better while continuing to drink. Only worse.

Although the drinking alcoholic may not be the least fortunate, the most in pain, or even the most hopeless of our species, he behaves like fallen humanity under a microscope. His faults are exaggerated even to the casual observer. He is irresponsible, self-centered, willful, deceitful, prideful, and, at times, disgusting. He provides an excellent example of the way in which the human experience can become distorted and perverted. His alcoholism affects every aspect of his life—physical, mental, emotional, social, financial, and many others as well—and by the end of the progression his life is a complete disaster, entirely due to alcohol.

If one chooses to follow the thinking of AA, however, it appears that alcohol is not the cause, but rather the symptom, of his disease. Alcohol is the agent, not the cause of his doom. The disease itself is actually centered not on the drinking of the alcoholic, but on his spiritual condition. It is true that his body responds to the physical consequences of drinking, and he may experience the progression of the disease in entirely physical symptoms up to, and including, death. Addiction to alcohol is, at the most basic level, physical. Acting out that addiction, however, is a spiritual malady, and the way out—the cure—is not physical in nature, because the individual cannot turn off the source of his longing using physical means. The longing is spiritual in nature, and must be countered by spiritual means.

It is quite possible that all members of the human race experience the sort of longing which, in the addict, leads to self-destruction (in the case of the alcoholic, by means of an ever-worsening physical disease). On the positive side, however, is the possibility that the spiritual remedy (which the alcoholic needs to stay alive) can be used by anyone who chooses to do so to the benefit of his or her spiritual well-being.

Once it has been established, even as a possibility, that addiction to alcohol is a spiritual malady which *involves* drinking, the way is clear to see a much bigger picture. Other addictions are similar, but instead of alcohol some other substance (for example, narcotics) or some other behavior (gambling, sex addiction) is involved. From this perspective, all addictive behaviors have a spiritual disorder at their center, manifested in a variety of ways, depending on the nature of the particular addict.

Spiritual diseases require spiritual remedies, and that is where the Twelve Steps provide a possible solution.

No one can become an alcoholic by willing it to be so.[6] Conversely, an alcoholic cannot become sober by force of will, whether his own or that of someone else. However, the process of becoming alcoholic is not clearly defined, and the ways in which alcoholism starts are as varied as alcoholics themselves. Normally, the craving associated with chronic alcoholism does not start at once, and is generally preceded by a long period of time in which the drinker actually enjoys the effect alcohol has on his personality. During this time the drinker still has some sort of choice, even though his choices are becoming ever more limited, until the lure towards active alcoholism becomes too strong to resist. The initial compulsion to drink feeds on the personality like a whisper deep inside the drinker's soul. At first he may not even hear it—at least, not very clearly. By the time the whisper grows into a raging tirade, there are no choices left. He is hooked.

Most often this progression takes a number of years, during which time the individual may indulge in a good deal of social drinking. Unfortunately, "social drinking" means different things to different people at different times and in different cultures. In some countries it is socially acceptable to drink with the intention of getting drunk. In others, drunkenness is a shameful and degrading behavior. There is an interesting contrast, for example, between the popular customs of Greece and Russia in this respect. In traditional Greek circles, drunkenness is regarded as very bad form, and among the clergy it is almost unthinkable. In Russia, on the other hand, laws had to be enacted to ensure that priests did not lie drunk in the streets—an indication, at least, that such an occurrence happened from time to time. Some religious groups shun the drinking of

---

6 It is said by those who know these things that a single use of heroin is capable of setting up an immediate addiction to that substance; that detail should be borne in mind when dealing with heroin and similar substances. On the other hand, the stronger drugs do not always cause the greatest addictions. In comparison with alcohol, nicotine is hardly as powerful or destructive, yet recovery from nicotine addiction is very difficult.

alcohol in any form, while others, including the Orthodox Church, place the drinking of wine at the very heart of their religious experience. These social and religious constraints probably make little difference to the development of alcoholic drinking, however, except that a sense of guilt and shame surrounding alcohol makes the progression more complicated and difficult.

After the novice alcoholic goes through a period in which he is aware that he has less and less choice as to whether he drinks or not, there follows, typically, a period in which the person cannot predict whether, at any given time in the future, he will actually be sober or not. Contrary to almost every piece of homespun wisdom, it matters little whether the person is a steady drinker or a binge drinker; it makes no difference whether he drinks beer or spirits, red wine or white, with or without eating. It makes no essential difference how much the person drinks at any one time. Some full-blown alcoholics never seem to drink more than half a glass of sherry (although this is, admittedly, rather rare). Others who are not alcoholic might regularly drink a fifth of whisky each day. According to the wisdom of AA, it does not matter what a person drinks (beer only, never mixed drinks), when a person drinks (never in the morning, only on Thursdays), how quickly a person drinks, or how much a person drinks. What matters is what effect the alcohol has on the personality of the person who drinks it. If alcohol becomes the main means by which a person is able to escape the present moment, that person is in serious trouble.

Rarely do people manifest the symptoms of alcoholism overnight, but it can happen. I knew an elderly lady some years ago who did not start drinking until she was advised by a doctor to have a glass of port (or something similar) in the evening before going to bed. She was then 72 years old. I met her in a treatment center when she was 75, by which time she had lost almost everything, except her life.

Not all heavy drinkers are alcoholics, and not all alcoholics are heavy drinkers. Alcohol is dangerous to both groups, however, and death is not interested in the individual's diagnosis. A drunken alcoholic behind the wheel of a car kills in exactly the same way as his nonalcoholic, heavy-drinking counterpart, and his victims are just as dead.

Some people appear to be alcoholic but are not. Some go through periods of dangerous and compulsive drinking in their late teens and early twenties, and then suddenly stop (if they survive) when they start to find responsibilities in life. Still others drink heavily mainly as a protest, particularly in cultures where alcohol is generally forbidden, or even to fulfill some unwritten rite of passage, as may be observed, for example, among college students in many countries.

When exactly a person slides from social drinking to the early stages of alcoholism is often not at all clear. Certainly it seems to have less to do with the amount of alcohol than with the disposition of the drinker at the time.

Medical research suggests that there seems to be a genetic predisposition in some people to become alcoholic. Anyone with one or more alcoholic parents might be thought to be in danger, although like everything genetic, the predisposition can sometimes skip a generation. It is then carried by people who are completely unaware that they have something dangerous in their genetic makeup which they are passing on to their offspring. Even then, the condition may only become apparent in one person, not in his brothers or sisters. There are recorded cases where no known genetic influence can be traced, at which point other possible causes, including psychological ones, have to be considered. There are, naturally, many possibilities, the most likely being that the condition we call alcoholism is actually due to one or more factors, some of which may be easy to measure, others not. Tracking the causes of diseases is never an easy task. One might think it obvious, for example, when lung cancer attacks a heavy smoker. However, not everyone who has lung cancer is, or has been, a smoker, and yet the cancer acts on both in exactly the same, destructive manner.

It is certainly true that the children of alcoholics have very special problems of their own. Many of them fear and hate drinking, since it is the cause of so much of what seems to be wrong with their lives; many of them are adamant that they themselves will never touch a drop of alcohol. Unfortunately, such a resolution does not always last forever, and very often they, too, are pulled into the destructiveness of alcoholism whether they like it or not. Incidentally, the Fellowship of Adult Children of Alcoholics also uses AA's Twelve Steps in their program of recovery.

Obviously, if someone who is born with the likelihood of becoming an alcoholic never actually starts to drink alcohol, the chances are that the person's alcoholism will never be diagnosed. It may be true that such a person demonstrates certain behavior patterns which could indicate the presence of alcoholism without the actual drinking, but the person with the inborn likelihood has to drink at some point for his alcoholism to be noticed and labeled as such. Finally, it may be true that some people even in this category actually dislike the sensation of drinking alcohol, and manage to beat the odds by refusing to drink very much of it, if any at all.

It does seem to be true that a prospective alcoholic generally has a strong physical constitution, since the body has to be reasonably healthy in order to tolerate the amount of alcohol which is usually required before alcoholism is able to take its normal course. The craving for alcohol is almost certainly due to a transformation that takes place in the brain, and this transformation is the result of the action of the alcohol drunk by the individual. The fact that most alcoholics seem to be able to tolerate alcohol rather better than non-alcoholics (and thus drink more of it) might be part of this process.

Just to complicate matters, there may be a psychological craving, unconnected with the physical craving, in the alcoholic's make-up; this means that even if one craving fails, there is a backup that pulls the person ever further towards addiction.

Once the physiological or the psychological craving is in place, the person has very little in the way of decision-making power to do anything about it. Instead, alcoholics who are just starting out often develop extraordinary forms of justification for their condition. A favorite ploy is to have a number of beliefs about alcoholism (kept in the recesses of the mind, never talked of in public) which always place the dividing line between the heavy drinker and the alcoholic somewhere beyond his own, particular behavior. Thus, he might believe that he cannot be an alcoholic if he only goes to bed drunk two nights a week. Later on, that number may grow, as his behavior deteriorates. Almost everyone has a vision of an alcoholic being the sort of person one finds dead in gutters, so if one is not dead in a gutter, one could not possibly be an alcoholic; at least, that is the way the thinking goes.

Alcoholism is progressive. It always gets worse. This is true during its active phase and, according to the experience of AA, it is true during the recovery phase as well. That is to say, the course of the disease continues to progress even in a sober alcoholic. This means that if someone starts drinking again after years of sobriety, he will experience symptoms which would be consistent with his condition had he been drinking alcoholically throughout the entire period. This belief is built on experience, not experiment. No sober alcoholic in the world would put this theory to the test for the sake of an experiment. Unfortunately such experimentation does occur in real life, committed by people who convince themselves that they are no longer alcoholic. The results are often fatal.

During the developmental stage of active alcoholism, behaviors tend to get worse and worse as the drug makes more and more demands. Mood swings become more common, and there may be periods of alcoholic amnesia. These episodes are sometimes called "blackouts," although here it simply means that the person forgets what he did or said under the influence of alcohol; it does not mean that he has to pass out. On the contrary, alcoholics sometimes get quite expert at living through blackouts. Certain functions of human behavior continue to work, at least at a certain level. It is not unknown for people to be able to drive a car with some degree of success while they are in a blackout. Indeed, some people seem to specialize in driving a great deal in this condition, waking up to find themselves in strange places, with no recollection of how they got there. In turn, this practice leads to one of the most bizarre and disgusting rituals performed regularly by alcoholics—going to the car in the bleak light of day, and checking to see if there are any signs of new bumps, dents, or (even worse) blood.

For some, driving while drunk may become a common occurrence;

for others, fighting while drinking may become normal. Some drunks simply sit in a corner and pass out. Others go out, looking for trouble. Behavior that is quite out of character may surface, particularly in the later stages of drinking.

Eventually, for some, hallucinations and a variety of unpleasant symptoms complete the picture, as the person slides toward insanity or death. This progression might take many, many years, with each stage hardly distinguishable from its predecessors. However, as already mentioned, it can happen remarkably quickly, to the greater astonishment of no one than the drinker himself.

A drinking alcoholic is absolutely isolated from the rest of the world. The most important relationship in his universe is with alcohol, and his own will is the most powerful entity in his sick universe. He is chained to the relationship with the drug that will eventually kill him. He hates the pain and the problems, the anger with which his life is shrouded, and he may hate the lying, the deceit, and the need to remember lies. However, he cannot envision his life without alcohol, because he is convinced that the drug is his only solace and consolation: it is his best friend, his lover, and his protector; it is his destroyer and it is his god.

By this stage in the progression of the disease, there is not much that is right about the alcoholic's life. At the core of his being there is a defect, which can be expressed in a number of different ways. One way that is obvious to most people is that the fullness of being a human being is realized in terms of our relationships with other people. In our individuality we are not complete; it is in our relationships that we come to the fullest sense of being. We cannot be sure of what it means to be "I" until we are able to recognize the "I"-ness of someone else.

In Christian theology, it is precisely this belief that gives life to our understanding of God. God is Trinity, and the individual Persons are Persons because they are in relationship—an eternal mutual expression of divine love, each for the other two.

At a more earthly level, we can see that the fullness of what it means to be human occurs when we communicate. The great works of art—painting, sculpture, and music—are great because of their ability to communicate. This is true even if the artists are anonymous, or forgotten—their "personhood" in communication is more important than their historical being, since they continue to live through their art. For example, I do not know who Beethoven was as a man, but when I listen carefully to his music, I know who he is as a person.

This entire area of human experience is lacking in the life of a drinking alcoholic. He finds it difficult to perceive any self in the entire world other than his own. Although his emotional range may be very wide—he may go from being extremely happy to being very sad (and quite often, morose) in a short period of time—he lacks reference to the experience of anyone else, or to any sense of moderation or subtlety. Indeed, subtlety is almost entirely lacking in the life of an alcoholic. His is generally an "all or nothing" world. There is no compromise, no rationality—just the pain of the present moment. And, in the thinking of the alcoholic, the pain of the present moment is what must be avoided at all possible costs.

This is just one of the many reasons why people who are in a long-term relationship with drinking alcoholics find life to be so difficult. Their biggest mistake is to continue to believe that they are the most important part of the drinker's life, and that they have a responsibility to care for the alcoholic, to save him from himself. It sometimes comes as a great surprise to such people to find out that they haven't actually been in a relationship worthy of the name for a long time, since the all-consuming and all-destroying relationship between the drinker and the chemical CH_3CH_2OH is the only one of any significance in the life of the drinking person.

Not only are relationships extremely difficult for the alcoholic to maintain; there is a consummate lack of communication within the alcoholic also. The human personality is of intricate and beautiful design, and there is a complex system of sharing experience and ideas within the personality. In the drinking alcoholic, these transmissions are severely disturbed, and thoughts and feelings may start to manifest themselves in all sorts of unexpected and unpleasant ways. Many alcoholics go for long periods of time without natural sleep—in fact, much of the time when their eyes are closed, alcoholics are actually unconscious due to the amount of alcohol they have drunk. The natural process of making, transmitting, and receiving dreams is severely disturbed. In the later stages of drinking, these inner communications sometimes surface during waking time. There can be instances where alcoholics hallucinate long before the well-known and often fatal condition called delirium tremens occurs. When this happens, it is as if the unconscious mind, with all its attendant fears, horrors, and dangers, emerges into the conscious part of the personality in an attempt to salvage something of its necessary function.

The feeling of total isolation experienced by the alcoholic, though not necessarily recognized by him, includes areas where normal people would not even think it possible to be isolated. For regular people, being conscious may not always be a wonderful experience, but at least it can be relied on. For the drinking alcoholic, becoming unconscious starts to be a welcome alternative to the pains of living. However, in the course of time, the unconscious mind of the drinker also becomes tainted with the pain and insanity of the conscious world. Closing his eyes no longer keeps the pain away, and there seems to be no way of keeping the insanity out.

As time goes by, the gap between intention and performance grows larger. It is normal for alcoholics to be all-or-nothing: something is either worth doing or it is dismissed as rubbish, nonsense, or something beneath contempt. And even then, the chances are nothing will happen. Most alcoholics live most of the time in a state of complete potential. They may be about to do something, they could do something, they may be thinking about doing something, but they rarely *do* anything, other than drinking. Planning looks wonderful and powerful, and contemplation looks helpful, but action is unusual. Many alcoholics have set out to write the best novel in the world with a blank sheet of paper and a bottle. Very often the bottle is finished before a single line has been written down. They attempt to take alcohol along with them on their path to fame and fortune, success and fulfillment. Unfortunately, alcohol is a disastrous companion, since it almost always robs the person of any sense of success at all. For every well-known alcoholic writer, there are probably several thousand others who have died trying to emulate his achievements.

Truth and honesty are no friends of the alcoholic. These are commodities which the rest of the world finds valuable, but which the alcoholic finds an embarrassment. Very often an alcoholic will automatically tell a lie rather than the truth, since in doing so he is actually able to control reality a little better, and he does not have to remember those difficult-for-the-unwary details called facts. An obvious difficulty for the alcoholic is that memory is impaired, particularly during periods of alcoholic amnesia. Trying to remember what lies have been told to which people, placed on top of alcoholic amnesia, leaves a sense of chaotic control which is nothing less than a foretaste of hell itself.

Even in early sobriety, recovering alcoholics may find that they still have the tendency to tell a lie rather than the truth, simply because it has always been easier to do so. To tell a lie is to create one's own reality—the greatest accomplishment of the alcoholic. To tell the truth means accepting *real* reality. Alcoholics hate to do that. An alcoholic will change and adapt all facts, figures, dates, promises, and vows, since everything about him has to serve the single purpose of the alcoholic—to keep his relationship with alcohol secure. Obviously, his situation sometimes involves some compromise, particularly when he is actively threatened by people in authority. However, it is not likely that he will put aside his main goal for long.

At a certain point in the progression of the condition, alcohol seems to ensure the rest and quietness of the alcoholic. Unfortunately, as the condition progresses, the numbing effect of alcohol seems to diminish, and in due course the alcoholic wakes up when he would much rather sleep through the worst symptoms of a hangover. This means that the time-span of the hangover is extended, and since an important part of the hangover is nothing more than the craving for more alcohol, the duration of the temptation is likewise lengthened. Drinking in order to stop the pain of hangover is a vicious cycle, and one which almost every alcoholic has to face at some time. Lying awake in excruciating pain at a time when one would really prefer to be asleep becomes common, and it is then that the alcoholic has to decide whether or not he can actually get through the rest of the day (which might involve a certain amount of black coffee and baths), or whether the sense of pain is so great that he has to start drinking again just to survive. It is in this way that binge drinking often perpetuates itself.

The progression continues even if the alcoholic does not have much money, or a regular source of alcohol. At times when it is necessary to drink simply because the pain is completely unbearable, the ability to make moral decisions disappears. The only thing felt is need, and the need is for the fix, and nothing can be more important than the fix. It takes superhuman effort to break this cycle even temporarily. To break it permanently is almost an impossibility.

If employable, the alcoholic will choose work to maximize the possibilities for his true aim in life. Of course, the individual is not thinking and acting at a conscious level here, and a great deal of the main motivation in his life remains hidden, even from himself. It is only when some other force causes him to defend his point of view that he might occasionally be brought face-to-face with the truth.

A drinking alcoholic is a person who is well acquainted with anger, since he lives in a world in which anger is the most common commodity. Through experience, he knows that the whole world *is* actually against him. His is not an ordinary paranoia, which is known and understood by the rest of the human race. His is a paranoia which is justified. A drunk can approach a perfect stranger and make an enemy just by eye contact. So much pity and anger is expended on most alcoholics during their drinking careers that they are often quite right in thinking that most people consider them good for nothing.

A drinking alcoholic cannot love, since the center of his world can never be another person. He can only reverence alcohol or the means of obtaining alcohol or the chance of being left at peace with his alcohol, no matter what sloppy and ill-kempt emotions try to persuade him otherwise.

His moral judgment is lacking, since he has no sense of good and bad, only of expedient and unwise. Because he lives for an all-elusive sense of satisfaction based on consumption, he has absolutely no sense of self-restraint, and self-control is the very opposite of his avowed aim in life. He has no patience, often because the only real moment in his life occurs when he can get to the next drink. As far as he can understand, his own will is all-powerful, and nothing and nobody is allowed to endanger that state of affairs. If there is one emotion which gets through his lead-lined defense system, it is probably fear. The alcoholic has fear coming from outside and fear coming from inside. This is due largely to the fact that the drinker cannot rely on alcohol to be the best friend, the guide and guardian that he would like it to be. Alcohol is altogether a false god, since it is not a person but a thing, and has no care or concern for the life of those it takes under its shadowy wing. It is also a depressant, and rewards the drinker with chronic symptoms of depression on top of the permanent physical pain involved with drinking too much.

The drinker knows treachery, and quickly gives up on loyalty. He learns to trust no one. He regards longsuffering as something for the idiots of this world. He does not even know what hope is, since his values only stretch toward immediate gratification, and hope requires patience.

One of the greater ironies is that the alcoholic is, surprisingly, very capable of self-discipline. However, this is not with a view to learning self-restraint or courage, but is entirely aimed at punishing himself. He can work at several layers of consciousness at once, and whatever his conscience has turned into within the haze of alcoholic thinking, it usually only appears in order to torment him with grief over his past behavior.

It would be a mistake to think that the alcoholic approves of his own behavior, even though he is entirely devoted to continuing it. He despises his behavior, he despises alcohol, and he despises himself.

It would also be a mistake to think that the alcoholic plays a purely passive role in his relationship with alcohol. He is actually in a state of constant war with it. Indeed, every time he takes a drink he is attempting to fight alcohol and win. However, as he learns over time, this struggle is fruitless and cannot be won. Yet still he continues, as if striking a square peg harder and harder will ultimately make it fit a round hole. He tries again and again to apply remedies to his life which have been tried so many times before and which have always failed.

For the drinker, humility and humiliation are synonymous. Courage might emerge as some sort of drunken foolhardiness from time to time, but that is all. Justice is dismissed as the province of anyone stupid enough to believe in the virtues of this life, and peace is an impossibility sponsored by fools.

For the alcoholic, there is no point in talking about willpower, since that is the very thing about him which is impaired. It is this fact—that his ability to make choices is impaired—which makes it difficult, if not impossible, for the alcoholic to take advantage of the sorts of methods that are traditionally employed to help people, and this is true at all levels of attempted treatment.

The most that traditional medicine can generally offer the alcoholic in any direct way is to make the drinking of alcohol a totally unpleasant and dangerous experience. This is done by administering a particular drug which reacts badly with alcohol, leaving the person feeling very unwell indeed. The theory is that as long as the drug is administered, the person will naturally choose not to drink alcohol. Unfortunately for alcoholics, this is rarely going to work in the long term, since such people often drink to the point where drinking is disgusting and dangerous, and they do that without the help of any prescribed drugs. Besides, the compulsion to drink is always stronger than any fear of consequences, and the temptation to do so has a timeless quality which cannot be matched by the administration of any drug.

Heavy drinkers who are not alcoholics may respond to the aversion therapy described above, at least for a while. It doesn't work for alcoholics, though, since it is expecting the alcoholic to make a rational choice based on evidence and good sense. If he were susceptible to even tiny amounts of either, it might work. But he isn't. So it doesn't.

It cannot be stressed too strongly: Alcoholics are suffering from something much more serious than a misuse of the human will, or a series of bad choices. They are actually suffering from a diseased will; they cannot make good decisions. No amount of effort makes any difference, since they have nothing to work with.

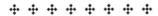

KINDNESS AND SYMPATHY ARE VERY OFTEN the most pernicious gifts that can be offered to an alcoholic. Both tend to give the message that the drinker need not have a sense of responsibility, given the circumstances of his life. The alcoholic picks up such sentiment as if he had a hidden short-wave radio tuned in just to that sort of statement. In the thinking of the alcoholic, any excuse for his drinking allows him to drink. In much the same way, any excuse for the overeater allows him to overeat, for the sex addict to act out, for the gambler to gamble, or the overspender to overspend. Any relaxation of the notion of total responsibility is enough to create a reason to wriggle through and do the behavior—not for its own sake—but for the feeling of relief it brings. It is not so much the taste of the alcohol, or even the effect of the alcohol that is so intoxicating. Rather, it is the freedom to "indulge"—to act without responsibility—which is more tempting than the human frame can bear.

Alcoholics spend most of their time being emotionally numb, and making sure that they stay that way. No wonder, then, that the newly sober alcoholic is not quite sure what it means to have a feeling, or what to do with a feeling when he gets one. If something bad happens to him or around him, the alcoholic typically finds someone else to take the blame, and (with equal fervor) makes sure that no matter what the situation, it is he himself who comes out as the victim of the piece. After an event like the tragedy of September 11, 2001, in New York City and elsewhere, alcoholics all over the world were no doubt proclaiming how they, personally, were harmed because of the events.

Early on, alcoholics dismiss as fanciful any sense of cause and effect in their relationship with their own bodies. They tend to view themselves in a very disconnected way—the person is disconnected from his own body, just as his own body is disconnected from every other. Each morning he may be surprised to wake up and find himself still in his body. The body is battered and in pain to be sure, but it is still there, ready to take more punishment, ready to be dragged a little nearer death.

The alcoholic lacks a sense that he is connected with the rest of the world, or even with the rest of the human race. This is not a concept which the Steps themselves use, but it does go a long way to explaining the predicament of the alcoholic. Everyone feels some degree of isolation in his life, to a greater or lesser extent. Just like paranoia, this feeling of isolation is a necessary part of the human being's repertoire for coping with the difficulties of life. In common with the other existential threats—meaninglessness, pain, anxiety, and death—an awareness of isolation makes us strong, independent. Indeed, all threats to our existence are important to us, no matter how unpleasant they may be, because they give us a sense of dimension, a sense of experience. For example, hunger is more of a natural state than the feeling of being full of food. If you do nothing, you get hungry. Hunger hurts, or at the very least, feels uncomfortable. At one level, hunger is necessary to spur us on to finding, preparing, and eating food. At a completely different level, however, it is useful to us because it makes us appreciative. A man who has eaten well at a banquet will discard a piece of bread as being unworthy of his attention. The starving man will find that same piece of bread entirely delightful, its taste exquisite.

Isolation teaches us to be independent, and to stand on our own feet. The alternative would be to be like sheep, or to be dependent on someone else to make all one's decisions. However, isolation at the level at which it is generally experienced by the alcoholic is far beyond that which might encourage him to be self-reliant. Rather it is a sense of being completely isolated, out of the usual arena of cause and effect. All information coming in has to be filtered through the ego, and that which does not fit is simply discarded. Disjointed and out of contact with the rest of the world, he feels too that his own personality is fragmented.

Listening to alcoholics telling and retelling their experiences during meetings, there is often a fairly close degree of similarity. What they describe is not just a sense of a loss of individuality—there is plenty to indicate that the alcoholic feels very much alone. Rather, it is a sense of having no inside at all—no "there" there. In an excruciating effort to be the king of the universe, he loses all sense of self. Think about the trick you can see at the circus where the magician has a lot of plates spinning on top of poles. He runs around, building tension in the act by allowing some plates almost to drop. For the alcoholic, his whole life feels like a lot of plates all on the point of falling down. In the end, the only release that can give him any comfort is to drown his sorrows and seek the oblivion of drunkenness. The balancing act between keeping all the plates spinning and falling into oblivion is precisely the predicament of the alcoholic.

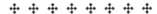

So far, we have seen the bad part of the story, and it can last for a long time, sometimes many years. However, so long as there is breath in the body, there is always the chance that the drinking alcoholic will get to the point where the pain is sufficient and the future hopeless enough to get him to make contact with AA. The whole process may involve one (or many) trips to treatment centers, the breakdown of marriages, loss of jobs, loss of dignity, and perhaps even a few trips to the hospital or the local jail, or worse. Eventually the few, fortunate ones will find their way to AA with no power left in them, no power to fight, no desire to go on. Such a person is in a state to be welcomed, to be accepted, and to listen. If he listens enough, for long enough, he may hear what he needs to learn.

Chapter 3

Life in AA,
Life in Recovery

Meetings

He who wishes to learn the will of the Lord must first stop listening to the demands of his own ego. Then, having prayed to God with faith and honest simplicity, and having spoken to the others in the group with humility of heart and no thought of doubt, he should accept what they have to say as from the mouth of God, even if their advice is contrary to his own wish, and even if those consulted are not very spiritual. For God is not unjust, and will not lead astray souls who with faith and innocence humbly submit to the experience, strength, and hope of the others. Even if those who were asked were brute beasts, yet He who speaks is the Immaterial and Invisible One.

This is an interpretation of what Saint John, the author of *The Ladder of Divine Ascent,* said in the seventh century (Step 26:111).

Given a different era and an entirely different group of people in an entirely different environment, St. John could be describing an AA meeting. In such a meeting, a person speaks and he is listened to. Then someone else speaks, and he is also listened to. Actually, advice is rarely sought, and almost never given, yet a great deal of learning takes place. If something is said that requires comment, another speaker will generally weave that particular piece of information into what he has to say, referring to mistakes he has made in his own life rather than rebuking the person who brought up the problem in the first place. This is not as convoluted as it may sound, since alcoholics tend to be rather unoriginal in the mistakes they make, and the same mistakes are likely to have been made by others in the room. In the end, what is shared at an AA meeting is the "experience, strength, and hope" of each person. When, in a meeting, somebody is unkind, knowingly or unknowingly, it is not uncommon for members of the group to rebuke the behavior gently but firmly, and not in an accusatory way. The atmosphere of an AA meeting is far removed from that of a dressing-down in the principal's office, the "you must try harder" speech of a beleaguered parent, or the mindless exhortations of a football coach.

Before getting to his first meeting, the alcoholic qualifies for everything that AA has to offer him, and the currency is pain—physical pain, pain of the heart, pain of living. In whatever form, pain is the constant companion of the drinking alcoholic. Sometimes it will cause him to do what is for him the most difficult thing in the world: to pick up the phone and ask for help. This represents the tiniest chink in his otherwise massive armor; considering his complete lack of emotional stability, the window of opportunity for doing such a thing may be extremely small. But miracles do happen.

Once he is in contact with AA, he will be introduced to two strong sources of support: the group (or the meeting) and the sponsor. By going to meetings and talking with a sponsor, he will have everything he needs for the real work to begin: doing the Twelve Steps.

Very often, once initial phone contact has been made, the alcoholic will be taken to a meeting by other alcoholics already in recovery. What he will see there is as obvious as it is unexpected. There are no closed-door secrets, no one sniggering and pointing, no unusual handshakes, no passwords—indeed, nothing out of the ordinary. He will be offered a cup of coffee (or tea), and will be greeted by people who look like . . . ordinary people.

It sometimes comes as a complete surprise to newcomers that recovering alcoholics look like normal people. Alcoholics do not naturally recognize other alcoholics, and if the only mental image a person has is that alcoholics live under bridges and drink boot polish, that image will undergo a swift and significant overhaul.

There are other things at the meeting which may surprise the newcomer. In AA there is no screening process. Indeed, there is no admission process of any sort. There are no forms to fill, no questions to answer. The only requirement for AA membership is a desire to stop drinking. The only initiation fee paid by those who start going to AA is the danger and harm they have inflicted on themselves through their use of alcohol. There are no professionals at the meeting—everyone there is a recovering alcoholic.

The newcomer is welcomed and encouraged to listen to the speaker, and to watch for points in the speaker's story which bear some resemblance to experiences of his own. Most alcoholics stop listening years before they stop drinking, so this in itself may be a novelty. Drinking alcoholics rank among the worst listeners in the world. Even if they can be engaged in a conversation, they rarely listen, since they are using the time when their companion is talking to think about what they want to say next. The form of communication favored by alcoholics is the monologue.

Listening is also the first thing an alcoholic learns to do on his path to recovery. From being a very bad listener, the alcoholic starts to listen, and starts to learn. In time, his listening skills may actually get better than those of normal people. Listening may never have been a human specialty, and in the modern world it is rare indeed. From a spiritual standpoint, this is particularly sad when one considers that *at least* half the experience of prayer consists in listening.

The new person may be only a few moments away from his last drink (at least, until now), and much of what goes on at the meeting may be no more than a blur by the time he comes to think about it. No matter. What is important is that he remember that he spent some time with a group of people who treated him kindly and with dignity, perhaps the first such encounter for a very long time.

The general pattern of an AA meeting runs like this: After a brief introduction during which the Preamble, the Twelve Steps, and the Twelve Traditions are read aloud, people speak, either on a theme that has been announced by the secretary as the theme of the meeting (the all-time favorite seems to be "gratitude"), or on some subject that is of particular concern to the speaker, or to someone else present at the meeting. Often, if there is a newcomer present, the whole meeting will be devoted to the First Step, allowing each of the members present to revisit his or her own experience of joining AA. In some of the bigger groups, newcomers may be encouraged to go into a smaller mini-meeting of their own, where their particular concerns will be addressed by members with some years of experience.

During a meeting, when someone is talking, the other members listen, and neither interrupt (called "cross-talk"—a definite no-no in AA etiquette) nor question the speaker. After the speaker has finished, he or she is thanked briefly, and then someone else talks. In small meetings, it may be normal for everyone to have a say. In very large meetings, only a few will do so. Each speaker either continues on the theme that has already been established, or talks about some issue of his own, almost always related in some way to the Twelve Steps.

In some meetings, the reading of AA literature is extended and becomes the main focus of the meeting. In others, there may be a guest speaker who talks for a major part of the meeting. In yet other meetings, the members present simply share "from the floor." In fact, almost all meetings end this way. As a rule, everyone who has a great desire to speak is free to do so, unless he is stopped from doing so by the length of the meeting, usually an hour or ninety minutes for the whole meeting. Notices are read, and a collection (called the "Seventh Tradition") is taken to cover the costs of the meeting, and to help towards the purchase of AA-approved literature, including packets of information that can be given *gratis* to newcomers. Most meetings end in prayer. Somewhat surprisingly, the prayer used is often the Lord's Prayer, although that is by no means compulsory, since the group itself can decide which prayers it wants to use. Another prayer, borrowed by AA long ago, is almost universal:

God, grant me the serenity to accept the things
    I cannot change,
Courage, to change the things I can, and
Wisdom, to know the difference.

Meetings are the heart of the AA experience; they allow the

members to discuss and share their experience of doing the Twelve Steps. It is a slow, yet thorough, process. Here the newcomer learns, by listening as well as he can to the stories of hundreds, perhaps thousands, of others, and he tells his own story in many, many different ways, many, many times over. Simply telling his story over and over again is an important part of the therapeutic process, and this is better achieved by telling it to lots of different people in lots of different groups, rather than forcing one person to listen to it time and time again.

In order to give some sense of scale to the required priority of getting sober, newcomers are generally invited to attend ninety meetings on ninety consecutive days. Any notion that a person can solve his problem on a part-time basis needs to be resisted at all costs, albeit gently. After a meeting, a particular newcomer was once invited by somebody present to attend another meeting in another place the following day. This the newcomer dismissed as overdoing things, and besides, he was a busy man. He did not stay sober very long.

Some people go to their first meeting, and afterwards they never drink again. Others are not so lucky. This is hardly surprising, since the individual is attempting to experience the most thorough transformation of his entire life, with the possible exception of his birth. Nevertheless, all are encouraged to continue going to meetings, since that alone is the path which promises some sort of recovery, even if the recovery is not immediate. Attending meetings drunk is not quite the abomination that some might consider it to be—the drunk person is certainly in the right place, and the other members are given a clear reminder of where they would be if they chose to drink again. Such a person is not regarded as an unwelcome guest (unless of course he has a long history of belligerent interruptions—and even then many groups show extraordinary amounts of patience). While members of the Fellowship will normally say that there is no point in speaking to someone who is drunk, nevertheless, if someone turns up drunk at a meeting, the other members tend to show a great deal of patience and understanding, knowing that the person in front of them is in need of the Fellowship more than anything else in the world.

Meetings in city center clubhouses or meetings in treatment centers with a lot of newcomers can be as enlightening as meetings in the suburbs, at huge conventions in big hotels, or at any other AA gathering, even though the vocabulary might be somewhat different. Speakers at meetings rarely use language intended to offend, but since all alcoholics share a background of less-than-gracious behavior, such things are not regarded as a serious breach of etiquette. The sense of fellowship between members of AA is very real, and strong friendships can result.

Members of AA who travel are quite likely to find out about meetings at their destination at the same time as they find out about hotel accommodation and travel arrangements. Certainly, it is always good for a member to check in with the local AA in a strange place. It sometimes happens that a member might go to a meeting in a foreign country, held in a language he does not understand, with people he has never met before, and yet still feel that he has an immediate sense of belonging to that group.

Members of AA find that it is not good practice to put each other on a pedestal. After all, all members of AA are one drink away from being a drunk. However, recovering alcoholics do show a great deal of tolerance to each other. It is wise to assume that all have suffered, all have lost something, and all have been oppressed. Once that is taken into account, it is no longer necessary to talk of it, or to treat anyone with anything like sympathy. On the contrary, members of the Fellowship often regard sympathy as a dangerous commodity, because it feeds into the very natural inclination of the alcoholic to view himself as a victim. Anyone who dares to say: "You poor thing" to an alcoholic (or any other victim) is encouraging that person to stay in his pain, because it brings him more sympathy. Empathy is required, not sympathy. This distinction is fine, but important. Empathy lets the suffering person know that his pain is understood, but does not reward him for it.

In recovery, the alcoholic finds that the various tools with which he is provided in AA are absolutely vital. The first piece of advice is, "Go to meetings." A second, invaluable, piece of advice is that during meetings he should pay attention to the things he finds helpful, and respectfully ignore the rest. A great deal might be said at meetings that he finds irrelevant, or even unhelpful. In that case, he is persuaded to ignore the parts he does not like. It is sometimes said, only partly in jest, that if a person enjoys all the AA meetings he goes to, he is not going to enough meetings. Meetings may be vital, but they cannot all have the thrill of instant sobriety all the time.

No one in AA has a position of power; all alcoholics are in danger of drinking again, no matter how long they have been sober. No one in AA has a monopoly on wisdom. Sometimes, indeed, the group needs to hear what a newcomer has to say more than anything else, although it is not necessarily helpful for the newcomer to know that!

Sometimes the terminology of AA is confusing to the population at large. For example, most people outside the Fellowship use the term "alcoholic" to apply to someone who is still drinking. They generally want to call someone who no longer drinks an "ex-alcoholic" or a "cured alcoholic." Not so in the Fellowship. Here people who haven't had a drink for years cheerfully give "alcoholic" as their title. The phrase, "Hi, my name is _____ and I am an alcoholic," is an acclamation, not a condemnation. It is a statement of power, not the admission of defeat.

Part of the potency of this word lies in the fact that the drinking alcoholic uses every possible strength at his limited command to push this label away, no matter how obvious it is to the rest of the world that he merits it. Concealing and dissembling take a tremendous amount of mental and spiritual strength; living this particular lie requires all the attention and effort the drinking alcoholic can muster. However, once this same alcoholic can stand up and say, "I am an alcoholic," the weight is lifted. The sense of relief at this moment is almost tangible, and it is not unknown for others in the room to start clapping or showing their approval in some other way, particularly if they have been watching the person attending the meeting for some time, without actually taking this all-important step. It is not uncommon for alcoholics to start attending AA meetings completely aware, on the one hand, that they need to do something about their problem, yet completely unable or unwilling, on the other, to admit that they actually have a problem. This sort of logic, common enough in AA meeting rooms, is somewhat baffling for the rest of the world. However, the newcomer quickly gets the hang of things as he sees others come in with exactly the same illogical frame of mind as himself.

The statement "I am an alcoholic" is packed with meaning. Although it is independent of the Twelve Steps, it nevertheless supports and complements the work the Steps encourage. First of all, it means, "I admit I have a problem." Any alcoholic who can say that is separated from the countless numbers of alcoholics who go to their graves rather than admit they have a problem. It also means, "I am a recovering alcoholic," even though the mystery of not drinking (one day at a time) may still not be part of his experience.

The statement "I am an alcoholic" means, "I am not god," or even, "I am not god, so someone else must be." In turn, since someone else is God, the drinker is free to let that Person do His job. The alcoholic is then free to be himself, and to find and settle into whatever the real God may have in store for him. This is a crucial stage in recovery.

From the first time on, the statement "I am an alcoholic" takes on another, important, significance. The title "alcoholic" is worn as a badge of honor, and it gives the bearer a sense of belonging in a group where everyone bears that title. "I belong to AA" means, in effect, "The heritage and the fellowship of AA belong to me." This is highly significant, particularly for someone who has known nothing but rejection for years.

It is helpful to bear in mind that the members of AA usually have nothing much in common with one another before they join the Fellowship, apart from the fact that they are all alcoholics. They come from every variety of social class, economic group, educational background, ethnic group, and religious persuasion. This last factor ensures that talk of "God" will be expressed in the simplest of terms, allowing each to use the word in a way he or she finds acceptable, without being offensive to others present. Any attempt to narrow the definition to a particular religious understanding, or to imply that there is a natural and obvious connection between what is said and the practice or belief of a particular religious group, is generally met with a comment to the effect that there are members of a number of religious beliefs present, and that what people say should reflect that reality. Naturally, there are likely to be some who call themselves atheists or agnostics, and will freely admit that their understanding of the word "God" (which in their case might as easily be expressed "God as we do *not* understand Him") may be most unsatisfactory from the point of view of some of the others in the group. Nevertheless, they, too, belong.

Sponsorship

AA members, particularly new ones, are encouraged to get a sponsor. It is the task of the sponsor to lead the person through the Twelve Steps, generally on the basis of a one-on-one friendship. This relationship is an important one, and is generally expected to last for some time. It is usual for the sponsor to have some experience in sobriety, though this has not always been the case; it is obvious that some of the people in the very earliest days of the Fellowship only had a few minutes more sobriety than the people they were sponsoring. Nevertheless, having an experienced sponsor is a distinct advantage, and choosing a sponsor is an important task. Some sponsors are very relaxed about the program, while others stick with fierce loyalty to the wording of the text, either contained in the *Big Book of Alcoholics Anonymous,* or in the *Twelve Steps and Twelve Traditions,* or in some other commentary on the Steps. However, all will encourage the people they sponsor to go to meetings, and to read AA literature.

A sponsor always mixes knowledge and the accumulated wisdom of the Fellowship with personal experience, because it is that experience, together with the promise of strength and hope, which is of primary importance to the person who is in recovery. The sponsor is *the* front-line defense against the possibility of drinking again, and provides important help in making the wisdom of AA available to the person being sponsored. In his turn, the sponsor provides his help, his wisdom, his friendship, his time, and his (sometimes almost impossibly limitless) patience as part of his service to AA, part of his action of paying back to the Fellowship what he owes, and in turn continuing to strengthen his own sobriety. Many sponsors will allow those they are sponsoring to call them at their homes, day or night. Most have learned (from experience) that it is important for an alcoholic to pick up a phone *before* he picks up a drink.

The parallels and differences between the task of the sponsor and the task of the spiritual father or mother will be described as the Steps themselves are examined.

The Structure of Alcoholics Anonymous

There is a great deal in AA that can be found in any other group of human beings. There is organization, a history, traditions (both written and unwritten), customs, and conventions. As AA grows, so its personality grows. Although there is a great deal of literature, most of AA's thinking is oral tradition. At each meeting it is possible to hear and rehear parts of this oral tradition—as widespread and as varied as the Fellowship itself, yet also coherent in its content, guided, as always, by the spirit of the Steps and the Traditions. When members, particularly newcomers, stray from the vision contained in the Steps and the Traditions, they are gently guided back to the original vision. There is certainly no insistence on the sort of uniformity of thought that one might expect to find in a cult. On the other hand, this is the Fellowship of people who know that their sobriety is safe only when they safeguard the unity of the Fellowship as a whole: personal recovery depends on AA unity.

Life in AA is not of a hierarchical nature, although there is organization. In the words of the Second Tradition, "Our leaders are but trusted servants—they do not govern." This is the spirit of leadership throughout the Fellowship, whether on a local, district, national, or international level. There are many jobs to do, and all are invited to participate. In most groups, there are suggested guidelines that someone should have completed a period of sobriety (often six months) before engaging in the active work ("service") of the Fellowship, particularly as an elected officeholder within the group; but that is in order to try to ensure some sort of stability. Each meeting elects officeholders (secretary, literature rep., treasurer, and so on), often for a period of six months at a time. Newcomers are encouraged to help with some of the domestic chores of the group, even though it is not uncommon to see a very senior, experienced member washing coffee cups or sweeping the floor.

Higher up in the organization, there is a certain amount of committee work to be done, and this tends to be done by people who would be good at sitting on committees in the world at large. There is a structure—local group, district, regional, national, and international—which is important to keep the life of the Fellowship going. However, the lifeblood of the Fellowship is not the international structure (since many AAs seldom if ever meet the Fellowship at that level), but the local meeting. In any given town, there is likely to be a wide variety in size, nature, and timing of meetings, so that as many as possible should have access to the message of AA. Women's meetings, young people's meetings, meetings for gay people—these are all available, and advertised as such in the local listings of meetings, or the meeting schedules often available as recorded messages on AA phone lines. Even here, however, attendance at a particular meeting tends to be not that exclusive, and in an emergency any meeting is better than no meeting.

Meetings are held in a wide variety of buildings—in church halls or basements, hospitals, and other facilities, sometimes even in private homes. A group may meet daily or weekly, or on certain days of the week. It is very common for recovering alcoholics to attend more than one group—it is generally possible to find a convenient meeting every day of the week—although they will usually acknowledge that one meeting (a "home" group) is the one to which they give greatest allegiance.

Groups have a high degree of autonomy. They are largely self-governing, and are self-supporting through their own contributions. Obviously, they need money to pay the rent for the room, and to pay for literature, some of which the group will have for sale. Local groups also give donations to the higher level of the organization (called Intergroups) which organizes the emergency phone line and some other services, usually on a citywide basis.

AA does not accept contributions from nonmembers, because it was discovered in the earliest days of the Fellowship that owning too much actually makes the mission of the Fellowship more difficult. Everything about the Fellowship is subservient to its avowed aim to help the alcoholic who still suffers. For the Fellowship, any other matter is an "outside issue" and detracts from the primary purpose.

Most large cities, and a great number of smaller ones in the United States, have clubhouses where AA meetings are held very frequently. AA does not own these clubs, even though all their members may belong to the Fellowship. At such a center, there may be a coffee bar or some other place where food is served, and where people can meet on a social level. Certain people in early sobriety find themselves with a great deal of time on their hands, particularly if they are not in full-time employment, and they often are not. Alcoholic drinking and full-time work do not go well together. Newly recovering alcoholics often need to learn social skills from scratch, and it is quite appropriate that they should do so from each other, since alcoholics tend to be very tough on each other, and do not readily allow for the sort of divergence from normal patterns which might eventually lead to a "slip"—i.e. a return to drinking. AA regards a slip as a somewhat involved procedure, and the signs of its occurrence are often more evident to others than they are to the drinker himself. It starts with what is called "stinking thinking" in the vocabulary of the Fellowship, and is rightly regarded as life-threatening.

Although AA is very good at what it does, there is sometimes disappointment over what AA cannot or will not do. AA is not involved with research on alcoholism at any level, and does not join social action groups. It cannot make any official diagnosis of alcoholics or alcoholism. AA does not provide money or welfare support to anyone, and does not run treatment facilities or provide counseling. It cannot even provide people with motivation to do the Steps, because that has to come from the individual concerned. AA is not affiliated with anyone at any level, yet it does try to cooperate with people who are regarded as supporters of the work of the Fellowship. Thus local groups will sometimes allow the secretary of the meeting to sign attendance cards issued by the courts, since many judges have discovered that sending people to AA is sometimes beneficial, and therefore sometimes "sentence" people to attend AA. The Fellowship has nothing to say about this policy, but it does not fight against it either.

One important feature of life in the Fellowship is that AA does not try to control its members, nor does it follow up on members who stop attending. AA is for those who want it, not for those who ought to want it. AA tries very hard to make its way of life available to all who need it, but none is forced to accept it.

AA does not regard the medical community or the scientific community as adversaries. On the contrary, the Fellowship seeks to cooperate with people who may be of assistance in their ultimate aim—to be available to the alcoholic who still suffers. However, the theories and practices of the medical community may be at variance with what AA thinks about alcoholism, and when that happens AA naturally stays with what it knows.

AA prints and distributes its own literature. There are several books, many authored by Bill W. himself, in particular *Alcoholics Anonymous* and *Twelve Steps and Twelve Traditions*, which are sanctioned by AA. Other books (for example, *Twenty-Four Hours a Day*) may be in common use among members of AA, but are not official AA literature, probably because they are too religious in tone. AA also publishes large numbers of pamphlets, because this is one of the most cost-effective methods of "carrying the message."

All members of AA who can do so are encouraged to read AA-approved literature, and most members of AA who have any length of sobriety are very familiar with parts of the Big Book, which contains the heart of AA's message. There are those members, too, who examine the Big Book (in particular) with great care, and quote it in meetings (often with page references) as the authoritative word of AA on any given subject. This tendency is sometimes particularly noticeable among those who may have a similar approach to the Bible. Other members may be less insistent on a black-and-white, literal view, and consider AA literature as a good basis for the development of personal thought.

There is a monthly magazine published by most national AA organizations, which is intended to provide a meeting between meetings for its members. In the United States it is called *The Grapevine,* and in the United Kingdom, *Share.* Alcoholics need constantly to revisit their problem, then revisit the solution, in order to stay sober for any length of time, and reading the magazine can help to do that when attendance at a meeting is not possible.

The organizational life of the Fellowship is successfully regulated by the Twelve Traditions, a list of which can be found in Appendix B on p. 206. Alcoholics Anonymous is a worldwide organization, but there is actually very little difference between the AA that might be encountered throughout the United States and Canada, and that which can be found in, say, Italy, Bahrain, or Samoa. The same literature is, of course, found everywhere, in a wide variety of languages, and the same themes and interests are the universal focus of its members. There may be minor differences in details, in matters like the customary length of meeting, or the choice of prayers; nevertheless, there is an overwhelming sense of unity and some uniformity in meetings throughout the world.

The fact of recovery from alcoholism is so central, so important in the lives of AAs that any factors which might naturally divide people tend to be regarded as having little or no importance. In fact, in certain parts of the world that are regularly in turmoil, the existence of AA tends to provide a real focus of hope in an otherwise hopeless situation.

What It Feels Like To Recover from Alcoholism

When, in recovery, sobriety starts to happen, alcoholics have to deal with the problem of coordinating body, mind, and spirit—after all, recovery is happening in all three areas at once. To the alcoholic this seems strange—the very idea that there might be some cooperation between himself and his body (let alone his soul) is such a novelty that he might think of it as one of the most bizarre effects of getting sober. The movement from chaotic disjointedness to unity and harmony is one of the first, yet one of the most lasting and important, sensations of sobriety.

Memory, for so long an enemy of the alcoholic, starts to become a friend. It is actually quite useful. Instead of intense physical and psychic pain, the individual begins to feel the quiet pleasures of "fitting inside" his own body. Tiredness and its accompanying sensations of relaxation re-establish themselves on first waking from sleep, a moment which in the past had always been accompanied by fear, dread, and (often) excruciating pain.

Thoughts start to come out in straight lines instead of being propelled, like so many convulsions, from the brain of the drinker. Things start to make sense, instead of providing an unending array of puzzling and disconnected thoughts. Objects stop moving around, and tend to be found where they were last put down. Keys, datebooks, pieces of clothing—they all tend to stay where they are put until they are required again. Clothes no longer bear unfamiliar stains; cars show no evidence of a half-remembered collision; food put into the oven gets taken out when it is cooked, not left to burn to a cinder, to be discovered by friend or neighbor or the fire department. Cigarette smoking becomes merely a threat to health and wealth, no longer a prelude to burnt clothing, burnt bedding, or burnt housing. Time starts moving in straight lines. The alcoholic starts to go somewhere and eventually arrives. When he goes home, he ends up at his own house; he doesn't wake up in the grimy reality of someone else's bedroom, or a police cell. He says that something will happen and there is a good chance that it really might. He starts to realize that words have a useful function, and are not just intended to push other people, with their hopes, their ideas, and their demands, away.

Sometimes, in sobriety, the drinker will find people actually do him acts of kindness propelled by nothing more than a spirit of neighborliness, untainted with pity. At the beginning he will not know how to react to this, since he will have to learn to trust. He is now in the ocean of give-and-take that constitutes human society, and most of the rules of that society are unknown to him. Gross manipulation and some sort of hoping for the best are the only tools he knows, and in sobriety they suddenly look out of place.

He may notice that people may smile at him for no reason—and there really is no reason, other than human kindness. He may not be dismissed out of hand any more, but society has many and different ways of refusing an individual's requests, and he will not be sure what is at stake when that happens.

Sobriety is never much more than a knife-edge. It is not a foregone conclusion, and cannot be taken for granted—it is a daily miracle. To live in the miracle, one has to be aware. Lose the awareness, and you lose the miracle. Lose the miracle, and you lose sobriety. Lose sobriety, and you lose all the blessings of life.

Recovering alcoholics have a very strong sense of the miraculous. Anyone who can remember a point in his life when he realized that he could not stop drinking—no matter how much he wanted to—will accept the gift of sobriety as something out of the ordinary, something which is above nature. Beyond belief. It is in that realm where the human mind cannot penetrate—the realm of faith—that the real work of recovery takes place.

Sanctity is not a requirement for staying sober, but willingness is. In fact, as people in sobriety get more adept at taking personal inventory, they tend to be more aware of how badly, rather than how well, they do in their daily lives. However, they also become more keenly aware of the power of God to forgive and to sustain that forgiveness. They are ever more aware that life is a gift to be treasured and used profitably—to be enjoyed, to be sure, but to be employed for some use, to find fulfillment of some sort.

Religious education provides one with religious knowledge. Sober living within the context of the Fellowship provides one with spiritual experience. Knowing "about" is clearly less interesting to most recovering alcoholics than knowing "that . . . ," particularly when the latter is approached with a profound sense of humility and gratitude.

In AA, complete abstinence from alcohol is seen as the only possible pathway to recovery from alcoholism, but recovery is seen primarily in spiritual, not physical, terms. This is true in spite of the fact that the Steps themselves are very practical in nature.

In AA meetings one commonly hears the old chestnut: Does

the alcoholic do the Steps to become sober, or does the alcoholic get sober in order to do the Steps? The somewhat mystical response would have to be that both are true, and both are at the very heart of what it means to lead a sober life, which for the alcoholic is the opposite of death, destruction, and insanity. "A sober life" may sound rather unattractive to most people, suggesting perhaps a lack of fun and a lack of relaxation or pleasure. However, to a drinking alcoholic, it actually presents a beautiful and wholesome alternative to insanity, destruction, and death.

After getting sober, life after death looks like a foregone conclusion.

Conclusion

AA is concerned with health. In its most obvious form, AA is concerned with physical health, because the ravages of alcoholism are often fatal. However, this is not where AA's main strengths lie. It would be obvious if AA were concerned with mental health, too. But here AA has almost nothing to say. What AA can provide, and has as the main function of its life, is the path to spiritual health. This spiritual health will incorporate and support improvements in physical health and mental health, but the underlying and overwhelming interest is in the spiritual realm. However, this notion of spiritual health is something which is not necessarily obvious to the outsider, and certainly not at all obvious to the alcoholic who stumbles into a meeting for the first time. Most will assume it is something to do with religion, but that assumption is only partly true. It is, in fact, a very powerful notion which underlies all the activities of life, and which provides multidimensional health—in terms of the relationship between the individual, his family, the rest of human society, the universe and all that it contains, and ultimately God. The key to understanding the importance of this spirituality is *anonymity*.

Chapter 4

Anonymity, Addictions, Denial, and Control

Anonymity

Anonymity is one of the least understood factors of life in AA. This is probably true because the term is applied to quite separate concepts at different times in the life of a recovering alcoholic.

When still drinking, an alcoholic tries to maintain a false façade. He tries to let the world know that there is nothing wrong with his life. Even if he is lying face-down in the gutter, he will, as likely as not, tell a passerby that he is fine. This is what denial makes him do.

The moment he starts to recover, or even considers what it might be like to recover, the average alcoholic is dreadfully afraid that people may find out. The thinking here is very devious. When he is drinking, the power of denial is strong enough to ensure that it does not matter whether people ever see him drunk in public. He will have all sorts of defense mechanisms for making sure that he does not, consciously, worry about such things, even when they are totally obvious to a very shortsighted person from a long way away. An alcoholic friend of mine worked as a teacher in the last years of his drinking career. During his last year of drinking, he had more than thirty days of absence from school. Under most situations this would likely mean that the person would be fired. Not so. The school seemed to believe—and the alcoholic was not sure he did not believe it too—that he simply had the flu very often that year.

The same alcoholic who is seen drunk in public may go to great pains to make sure that nobody finds out that he is attending his first AA meetings. The logic is simple. Once he starts going to AA, he has to admit that there is a problem. While he is still drinking, he can use denial (both his own and everyone else's) to pretend that there is no problem.

For this person, the whole importance of anonymity is that he should not be identified publicly as having a problem. Among all the factors that might make him suspicious or unwilling to attend his first meeting, anonymity is likely to be one of the only things which he finds attractive. He may still park his car many blocks away from the meeting and disguise his walk as he makes his way there, shielding his face from those driving past. For him there is a great deal of shame in admitting that he has a problem.

Once recovery is underway, however, anonymity starts to have another function. It allows him to be a real person. In most groups, and in most situations, he will be known by other members of AA simply by his first name. Indeed, AA members often have no idea of the full names of people that they may have known well for years. Thus, the identity of each individual is very simple. He is no authority figure, and has no history. He is simply . . . whatever his name is. This allows him to go through the initial periods of recovery with something like a cocoon. He does not stand for anything, does not represent anything. He can make mistakes if he needs to, even stupid ones, and no one will point a finger. He is just another drunk trying to get well. Whatever perfectionist tendencies he may have (and most alcoholics have a great number), he learns during this stage to welcome his anonymity, because it puts his task in perspective. He does not have to change the world in order to get sober. He can be himself. He can sit back, and just BE, in a sense, for the first time, and enjoy the freedom of a world in which he is not God.

Later still, anonymity has an entirely different function. Basically, when a person is doing anything in AA, he does so anonymously. This has the function of taking the ego out of whatever he is doing, thereby allowing whatever the action is to be for its own sake. In normal life, almost everything everyone does has a motive. By embracing anonymity, the individual learns to start doing what he is doing motivated by nothing more than the pleasure of doing it—in effect, he starts to be authentic. For an alcoholic, even the smallest possibility of being authentic is very attractive indeed.

Anonymity also has the function of strengthening a person's identity with the rest of the Fellowship. An anonymous person entering a room of anonymous people finds a sense of belonging in that fact alone. The fact that he is trusted with the anonymity of everyone else who is present becomes a source of great comfort to someone who has not been trusted for years.

It sometimes happens that anonymity has its wilder side, although it is almost always a cause for humility and gratitude. Coming across one's boss, one's doctor, or one's student, perhaps a film star or even another family member, can bring a considerable amount of spiritual contentment; every person in the Fellowship is safely wrapped in anonymity.

There is another, highly significant, yet mystical element to the whole thinking behind AA's anonymity. In the course of the Steps, God Himself becomes anonymous. God has to enter the veil of anonymity, since it is only in that form that He can be accepted by the alcoholic. God meets the alcoholic in the only way that the alcoholic is prepared to meet Him.

Sin and Addiction

When I was staying at a monastery on an island in Greece, I sometimes saw a man who was obviously the island's drunk (that is, excluding all the non-Greek residents of the island, many of whom seemed to have severe drinking problems). He was a small man, and the smell of ouzo (his downfall) was difficult to disguise, even in the open air and from some distance away. It struck me as both sad and pitiful that some of the other locals went out of their way to make his life miserable. Sometimes they would purposely get him drunk (or more drunk) so they could taunt him. Their sense of fun was a disgrace, but not (I think) that unusual. The presence of a drunk in a community makes everyone feel secure, because each person knows that no matter what happens, he or she will never be the laughingstock of the community—that place is already taken.

Under most circumstances, sick people are not punished for being sick, and in the modern world sick and disabled people are much less the objects of prejudice and unkindness than they have been in the past. In the Gospel, Jesus states quite specifically that a person born blind is not being punished either for his own sins, or

71

for the sins of his parents, a point of view which the disciples obviously considered to be normal. In a world where there was no obvious cause for something like, say, leprosy, the idea that a sick person was being punished for his own wickedness (or for someone else's) was not that outlandish. Even today, people with life-threatening disorders may sometimes be tempted to wonder if they are not being punished for something. Since no one is without sin, it is always *possible* to attribute illness to some cause of this nature. The general view in the Gospel—that such conditions have, as a purpose, the greater glory of God—is not always acceptable to us when the conditions are not accompanied by healing miracles.

When it comes to considering mental health, humanity is usually willing to concede that acts committed while someone is obviously insane are of a different nature from other, more straightforward, crimes, and such acts are usually dealt with in a way different from the way they would be treated if the person committing them were known to be in a right state of mind.

For the drinking alcoholic, the picture is not necessarily that straightforward, however. Most people coming across a drunk person will not automatically think of that person as being sick, even though they may concede that he is suffering from a disease. On the contrary, many people automatically assume that a drunk is a bad person, dangerous to others and to himself.

The first time I can remember seeing a drunk man was when I was very young. I went with my father to visit some relatives in Surrey, and while we were there we drove through a town that had a river flowing through the middle of it. At one point my dad stopped the car (an old Austin 7), got out, and started running, calling to me over his shoulder to stay where I was. Apparently he had noticed a very drunk man staggering somewhere near the river bank, and he was seriously worried that the man might fall into the river. Apart from the fact that my father shouted for a policeman, I cannot remember anything else about the incident. Certainly the whole situation terrified me, and I came away from the experience thinking that it was a good idea to stay away from alcoholics.

Looking back, I now doubt whether the man would have fallen

in the water. Either drunk people have a very strong sense of self-preservation, or their guardian angels are working overtime to keep them safe.

If someone commits a crime while insane, most legal systems allow for some leniency to be shown that person. The criminally insane are usually locked up rather than executed, and many penal systems have psychiatric prisons just for that purpose.

No one would doubt that a drinking alcoholic is insane. Even the alcoholic himself feels insane a good deal of the time. However, part of his insanity arises from the fact that he refuses to take responsibility for his own actions. Put another way, it is likely that by the time a person is drunk, his insanity is obvious to everyone. However, when an alcoholic is sober, it is unlikely that most people would find him insane, until that point where he picks up the first drink.

The thinking of AA has little to say about the morality of acts committed by an alcoholic while he is drunk. Such questions are the realm of lawyers and courts. However, the Steps are plainly worded to suggest that recovery involves the alcoholic dealing with the things in his past which he has done wrong. Steps Four, Seven, Eight, and Ten all focus precisely on things he has done wrong. He is encouraged to face up to his past, and, where possible, to make amends.

Within the Fellowship, the alcoholic is taught that he is held responsible for the consequences of picking up the first drink; he is also taught that there will be times when nothing less than the power of God will stop him from picking up the first drink. This is both paradoxical and crucial. On one level he may express the idea that no one ever forced him to drink; if he drank it was by his own choice. On another level, he acknowledges that to leave alcohol alone requires much more power than he, alone, can muster, and that nothing less than the direct participation of God will suffice to bring that about.

After the first drink, the responsibility of the alcoholic is a moot point, since his thinking is automatically impaired. However, insofar as he is responsible for taking the first drink, he is always responsible for his subsequent actions, even those which he may not remember once he becomes sober again.

The anguish of guilt is almost always part of the condition of alcoholism, although it may not be very apparent to the outsider. For this reason, it is always important for the alcoholic to come to terms with his past wrongs, or the day may come when the only way to relieve the pain of guilt is to drink, setting the whole cycle in motion once more.

There is every indication in the Twelve Steps that no matter how bad an alcoholic has been, forgiveness is still available for him. Furthermore, that forgiveness will not only take the form of removing the guilt for past sins, but may also involve the individual being freed from the shortcomings that led to the sin in the first place.

If anyone were to suggest to an alcoholic that he is simply sick, and not responsible for what he is doing, that action would be no act of kindness at all. Responsibility is the antidote to what ails the alcoholic.

Human nature, however, runs in a different direction. As a rule, what we want in an ideal situation is to have as much authority as possible, with as little responsibility as possible. In this regard, the drinking alcoholic simply amplifies the tendency of human nature in general. He wants control, but not responsibility. Unfortunately, control without responsibility is, in the end, a vile thing, and we can see evidence of that fact in the more barbaric episodes of human political history. Responsibility is the very element that is required for sane and spiritual living.

Viktor Frankl, a philosopher and a survivor of the German concentration camps of the Nazi era, is said to have made a comment that the United States was in need of another statue, to balance the Statue of Liberty in New York harbor. Perhaps one day there will be a Statue of Responsibility erected in the San Francisco Bay in order to complete the picture.

I once met a man who had just been released from prison after eighteen years' incarceration for a murder he had committed during an alcoholic blackout. The first thing he did on his release was to attend an AA meeting. In fact, he had arranged for other AA members to go to the prison to pick him up. When the time came for him to speak during the meeting, he chose "gratitude" as the topic. I do not know what happened to him after that meeting, but I feel it is safe to assume that he did not go out and get drunk.

An alcoholic has a compulsion to drink, and one which he can resist only by the grace of God. However, he is also responsible for the consequences of picking up that first drink, particularly once he knows that sobriety is an option. It is for this reason that one often hears the comment that although AA may not stop someone drinking immediately, it certainly spoils that person's drinking from that point on.

The first drink for the alcoholic actually represents everything from the first sip to eventual death. The same is not always true with regard to human life unaffected by alcoholism. For a regular person, the first sin does not inevitably lead to the second sin, although it may. Certainly it could be argued that committing one wrong action makes it easier to commit a second—either because it does not seem so bad the second time, or because after a while a particular sin might actually set itself up as a habit. Once something has become a habit, it is more difficult to correct. However, the internal struggle of a nonaddict in trying to shake a habit pales in comparison with the struggle of an addict attempting to rid himself of his addiction. If addiction were simply the same thing as a habit, it would be called a habit, not an addiction.

Although addiction has been around for thousands of years, several factors may make it more prevalent in the modern world than in the past. As a race, we now have access to knowledge and ability which those living in biblical times, or even in the time of the Fathers of the Church, could only dream of. Nuclear bombs, the contraceptive pill, life-support systems, the welfare state, afflu-ence, and a seemingly limitless development of technology may have given all of us a misshapen view of our own importance and our own power. When we challenge God today, we do so at a much more sophisticated level than did our ancestors, and even though our own Towers of Babel may in the future look ridiculous to our descendants, they look pretty challenging to us. It is possible that an imbalance in the way we view ourselves is directly responsible for the condition we know as addiction, and that our modern sense of power and security encourages us into a false sense of autonomy and self-determination which lies at the heart of that condition.

It may be a mistake, though, to assume that this phenomenon is limited to the postindustrial age. Saint Paul describes a particular situation like this: "I do not do the good I want, but the evil I do not want is what I do. Now if I do what I do not want, it is no longer I that do it, but sin which dwells within me." This is a perfect description of an addiction: there is a tendency to sin that dwells within the human personality, and because of it nothing good can result.

Saint Paul is not explicit about what he is describing here, and it may be unlikely that he is referring to addiction in particular. It is by no means certain that he would have understood the term in anything like the detail we have in the modern world. However, the question that he may be pondering—that our tendency to sin is something like an addiction—may be a further reason to look at the Twelve Steps with great care. If they can be used in treating one sort of addiction, they might well be used in treating an addiction of quite a different sort.

Sin itself may be nothing more than an addiction.

Denial

It is often said that the main and first symptom of alcoholism is *denial.* This presents the rest of humanity with something of a problem, because the person who says, "I do not have a drinking problem," and is an alcoholic, sounds exactly like the person who says, "I do not have a drinking problem," and is not an alcoholic. This makes the diagnosis of the condition rather difficult.

Denial is much more than lying, although there is an obvious element of that involved. Denial also involves the failure to maintain integrity in a difficult situation.

If anyone were to ask a drinking alcoholic how his life was going, he would likely hear an immediate response of "fine" or some other platitude. According to AA wisdom, drinking happens in three stages: impulsive, compulsive, and repulsive. The alcoholic's reply would likely be the same at each of the three stages. If you ask him if he has been drinking, he will reply "no" even if he has a glass in his hand. If you offer to give him some help, he will likely tell you that he doesn't need any help, especially from you. "Mind your own business and leave me alone" is one of the kindest things an alcoholic is likely to say under these conditions. "I am okay, I am all-powerful, I am in control." These are the lies the alcoholic lives with, since anything else would be to admit that there was a problem.

Denial comes in all shapes and sizes, some more perverse than others. Any sort of leader who thinks he is incapable of making a mistake is in denial, and those who confer honors and dignities on him as if he were infallible are also in denial. A person who is partially sighted yet insists on driving a car without glasses is in denial. Someone who refuses to acknowledge the reality of something important in life—death of a spouse, having a dangerous disease— is in denial. Pretending that we are invincible and will live forever is denial.

Denial does not only belong to the alcoholic himself. An alcoholic once attended a funeral in a total blackout. He had no recollection of being present at all. Even so, after some careful enquiry, he managed to convince others who had been present that he had been unwell that day, and everyone seemed to believe him. Denial is sometimes stupid and degrading, but it is often easier to handle than the truth.

Denial starts as a coping mechanism. Coping is what we need to do to get through a difficult situation, and very often when we start doing something just to cope—just to get through—we are reluctant to let go of that behavior after it is no longer necessary.

When I was about seven or eight, I sprained my ankle. I was playing in our back yard, and I tried to jump, but I did so without taking much care. Instead of landing on a level surface, one of my feet landed on a brick. I remember a great deal of pain, and eventually I was taken to a hospital on the bus. I remember that I was quite disappointed when I found that I had only sprained my ankle, and not broken it. A broken ankle sounded so much more romantic.

However, when I returned to school some time later I was allowed to go in to lunch ahead of the other children; I did not have to wait in line, because standing was quite painful for me.

Several weeks later, after the cast had been removed and I was no longer using crutches, I went in to lunch early, just as I had done in the preceding weeks, hoping that no one would notice. One of the lunch supervisors (called, somewhat graciously, "dinner ladies" in Britain) told me to get into line with the other children—my need to come in early was no longer valid.

I was crushed. My denial had been challenged, and I hated it. I was no longer special.

Occasionally one will come across forms of denial whose task is to make an otherwise impossible situation possible. For example, I had an elderly aunt who grew quite senile as she grew older. She adopted a number of habits that were distressing—particularly when we were out in public. In a restaurant, for example, one of her favorite things to do was to eat everything on her plate (she had been taught in childhood never to waste anything, and she made no attempt to adjust this adage in later, more affluent years); but having done so, she would proceed to lick her plate clean—much as a child might do. Since her short-term memory was almost nonexistent, there was very little point in arguing with her or trying to stop her, because, at some significant level, she thought that she was somehow helping. Thus, we family members would simply pretend nothing was happening. Other people in the restaurant might have been aghast as we sat there, pretending nothing strange was going on— but that was about the only course of action open to us. Anything else would only have made the situation worse.

If, however, any one of us around that table (apart from my aunt) had actually believed that what was going on was normal, that person would have been in terrible trouble, and in need of fairly immediate therapy. That person would have rejected God's reality, and replaced it with my aunt's reality. Such a person is called a code-pendent, to distinguish him from the person who replaces God's reality with his own reality, who is the addict. It may be there is a little bit of codependent and a little bit of addict in us all.

Thus, though not all denial is unacceptable, it is certainly necessary to raise it to the level of free choice before it is safe to leave it in place. Denial is at its most dangerous when the person who is actually involved in it has no idea that he is in denial.

The way AA copes with the problem is that it does not ask the alcoholic if he has a problem. It certainly does not ask if the alcoholic is living in a complete mess. The answer to both those would be an automatic and definite "no." Instead, it poses a very unthreatening question: Are you powerless over alcohol? Is your life unmanageable? These represent the thinnest of all possible thin wedges, which allow the alcoholic to pass from denial (in which the downward path of the disease is ensured) to a position of integrity where recovery can start.

ONE FORM OF DENIAL I HAVE COME ACROSS on a number of occasions is that Orthodox Christians with a drinking problem try to avoid going to AA on the grounds that AA is not Orthodox. I would encourage such people to go to meetings anyway. They will find that they are able to take their Orthodoxy with them (to the extent that they need to), just as others take their own religious traditions with them. Indeed, the richer the religious diversity in an AA group, the more that group is likely to be able to help other newcomers. Remember, AA is not a church, and AA is not a religion. The focus of every single meeting is sobriety, and that is what you need to go to find. If there is anything in the meeting which you really find offensive from an Orthodox standpoint, discuss it with your parish priest. If you still find that you are resisting AA because it is not Orthodox, you need to consider whether this is not perhaps an excuse.

✤ ✤ ✤ ✤ ✤ ✤ ✤ ✤

THE ANSWER TO DENIAL, provided by the first three Steps, is summed up in the following affirmation: "I cannot, God can, and I am going to let Him." It destroys denial at every level.

Chapter 5

Spirituality
and Religion

MOST PEOPLE, WHETHER THEY ARE RELIGIOUS OR NOT, use the words "religious" and "spiritual" as if they referred somewhat vaguely to the same thing. Thus the expressions a "religious" person and a "spiritual" person can be regarded as having more or less the same meaning.

In the thinking of AA, the difference between the term "religious" and the term "spiritual" is so great that the words could not possibly be confused. While the two terms are related, they nevertheless refer to two separate concerns, and this difference is crucial to AA's mission.

It is the sole aim of AA to be able to help the alcoholic who still suffers; it does not seek to impose its views on anyone, nor does it try to convince anyone of anything. AA does not seek to be in dialogue with anyone, unless it is with a view to passing on the message "to alcoholics who still suffer" who might be reached in places near and far. What AA does is extremely difficult, and in order to be successful it has to keep its mission in very sharp focus and constantly to limit itself to the task in hand. It was not established to educate the world about alcoholism, but to carry the message of sobriety to alcoholics who are still drinking.

AA does not attempt to educate anyone except its own members. However, if an outsider is going to understand what AA is trying to do, it is necessary to understand the basic definitions of AA's philosophy and the way that AA uses them. Otherwise, the significance of the program of recovery will never be fully understood. Those who wish to use the Twelve Steps for their own personal development need to be aware of some of the issues so that they can make up their own minds.

The life and practice of the Orthodox Church form a cohesive whole with the doctrine, official prayers, Scriptures, creeds, and canons that both enshrine and regulate her life. Within the Church there is a seamless connection between what is prayed and what is believed, and this holistic experience means that, under most circumstances, it is not necessary for anyone to make a distinction between religion and spirituality.

However, for AA to be able to fulfill its task, and to make its message available for all who need it, such a distinction is essential.

In the most basic terms, here are some statements many members of AA would find acceptable:

Religion and spirituality are two allied concepts, yet each has a different focus:

- Religion is concerned with the Person of God; spirituality is concerned with what God does.
- Religion has an important historical dimension; spirituality is most concerned with the present moment.
- Religion often has a speculative quality; spirituality is entirely practical.
- Religion focuses on God's relationship with humankind; spirituality focuses on a person's relationship with God.
- Religion is concerned with God's relationship with the universe; spirituality is focused on the way a person sees his own place in the universe.

To make sure this discussion does not become too theoretical, it will be necessary to place this thinking in an everyday context.

When the alcoholic turns to God, he meets an old adversary. The prayers of the alcoholic, long uttered in the despair of loneliness, are unanswered—at least in a form he is prepared to accept. The resentments he has about God, and most alcoholics have many, make it very difficult for him to encounter God, even if he were free of the alcoholic haze. Whatever notions he has about God from his childhood, from his upbringing, from his adolescence, they all need to be relinquished, because—like everything else about the alcoholic—they have become part of his disease.

Addiction in general, and alcoholism in particular, display a fundamental breakdown between the notion of self and the notion of God—even a breakdown in any sense of connection between the self and the rest of the universe. Any vague awareness of being a part of the universe is something the alcoholic has lost. He feels totally isolated, and he has no sense of the cause-and-effect idea that seems to constitute a part of everyone else's worldview. No matter what he does, the life of the alcoholic seems to get worse. He tries, and things get worse. He does not try, and things get worse. Sometimes, he finds that the harder he fights, the worse his life gets.

In order for him to get better, all his thinking, including his thinking about God, needs to be discarded and built up again from scratch.

The act of discarding everything the alcoholic *thinks* he knows cannot be done in a straightforward manner. It is not possible to remove his brain, clean it out, and replace it. Even the *possibility* of doing such a thing is remote, because the alcoholic will fight against it at every level. In the reality of the alcoholic's life, there is nothing reliable, nothing benign, nothing likely to afford comfort; his is a world in which just to stay in the pain makes it necessary to have cast-iron control over every aspect of his life. You cannot tell a man who is holding onto his reality with something rather more than grim determination that he simply has to let go. To him, that course of action looks suicidal. You might as well tell him to stop breathing.

What you can ask him to do is to admit that his life is unmanageable, and that he is powerless over alcohol. Strangely, *that* he is able to do, and the diseased ego lets go of the pretense of playing god. This is Step One. Of all the possible combinations of all possible words in the English language, these two expressions may be the only ones which allow the alcoholic to loosen the death-grip around his own throat.

At this point anything else might be used to substitute for the diseased notion of God—*anything* that is not the diseased ego of the alcoholic will do, any power that is outside the control of the alcoholic is acceptable. Step Two is a journey ("came to believe that a Power greater than ourselves could restore us to sanity"), and this point marks the beginning. By the end of Step Two, God, stripped of all the alcoholic's false notions, clothed in His own anonymity, is there by the person's side, ready to lead him back to sanity. That sanity consists in the individual turning to this anonymous God and giving Him his will and his life. That is Step Three.

When seen in hindsight, this process is all the more beautiful, because having arrived at Step Three, even the alcoholic can see that God has been participating in the process all the way through. Nevertheless, God allows the alcoholic to make the decisions, since that is the only way he is prepared to participate at all.

IN ORTHODOX THEOLOGY there is a very strong awareness about who God is—the Father, the Son, and the Holy Spirit. However, dividing the qualities of God into "what God is" and "what God does" is not unknown in the tradition of the Orthodox Church. In the fourteenth century, the theological tradition of St. Gregory Palamas made a similar distinction between the essence of God ("what God *is*") and the energies of God ("what God *does*"). The context of St. Gregory's work is entirely different from the present discussion, but the similarity of thought is there, nonetheless.

There is another, important area in which there is a similarity between the thinking of AA and the theological tradition of the Orthodox Church. The theological expression used to describe the descent of the Word of God into human form is called *kenosis*, the Greek for "emptying." The Word of God, co-eternal with the Father from before the beginning, "emptied Himself" in order to become a human being and fulfill His divine mission some two thousand years ago.

In AA this process is taken one stage further. It was discovered that God is capable of emptying Himself even further, for the sake of participating in the recovery of the alcoholic. In this recovery, the alcoholic learns to put aside his ego and start to realize that his finest qualities rest in his becoming anonymous. However, God also participates in this action. He also clothes Himself in anonymity, and becomes "God as we understood Him." He is prepared to subject Himself to the understanding of the person to whom He comes, for the sake of showing compassion to that person. This action of supreme condescension is the only way this could be effected. Anonymity is like a tent. The alcoholic enters the tent of anonymity, certainly, but God also enters the tent; there the meeting takes place, the confrontation, and the miracle of recovery can begin.

The God that the alcoholic meets in recovery will grow in the alcoholic's awareness throughout his practice of the Steps. In a sense the "God as we understood Him" of Step Three may not bear much resemblance to the "God as we understood Him" by the time he reaches Step Eleven. However, what is crucial is that the view of God should not be limited by the imagination of the alcoholic, since to be effective in the life of the recovering alcoholic, He has to remain separate from, and outside the control of, the alcoholic's will.

Recovering alcoholics include a fair number of people who have a good deal of religious training. These often find it difficult to come to terms with the fact that they have to strip down their notion of God. There is no point in having a technically brilliant vision of God if that God is not able to provide the alcoholic with life-giving sobriety. The old thinking, no matter how well-developed, must be discarded, because it did not work. In practice, this means that people who may be trained in theology suddenly find themselves having to be prepared to discard everything they know in order to learn about God from a group of uneducated recovering alcoholics.

This is what is meant by the often-repeated story that if alcoholics are unable or unwilling to believe in a power greater than themselves, they can choose something (or even someone) that can take the place of that concept. Hence the invitation to choose the coffeepot or a redwood tree as one's higher power. Obviously no one is seriously suggesting that the coffeepot is actually the Lord of the Universe or the Savior of the World. However, for the alcoholic to make that all-important transition, it does well enough for a start.

ONE OF THE LEAST SPIRITUAL WAYS TO LIVE is to attempt to avoid the present moment. Our alternatives are limited to two: to live in the past or to live in the future; sometimes we choose them both at once.

Attempting to live in the future is a very common phenomenon. It probably stems from a fairly obvious and common set of behaviors associated with looking forward to things in the future when one is a child. Personal power and responsibility in children is of a very low order, and thus looking forward to growing up very often equates to looking forward to being taken seriously, looking forward to being allowed to make one's own decisions, and so on. Thus, one looks forward to finishing school, or starting work, or getting married.

Living in the future allows us to pass through the present moment without being too affected by it. We put up with discomfort, in a million forms, for the sake of a better future. It is actually possible for people to base their entire lives on such a model. Unfortunately, as often as not, once one has reached the thing that one so eagerly awaited it is, in some sense, disappointing, and thus it is necessary to move one's target even further ahead.

Once the coping mechanism of living in the future is in place, it is very difficult to adjust it, or to stop it altogether. Life becomes a process of finding things to look forward to—thus avoiding the present moment at all costs. This very often goes on even when the present moment is actually quite pleasant. The danger exists, however, that the present will bring pain—boredom, feelings of inadequacy, and so on—and so it is avoided.

Eventually, a stage of life arrives when the individual realizes that his best days, and most of his opportunities, have already passed. At this point the individual tends to stop living in the future, and gradually starts to live in the past instead. The period in the middle is called "middle age" for good reasons.

Living in the past is equally difficult to alter. Naturally, this is more likely when people are a little older, and actually have something in their lives on which to look back. However, like its partner, it is an avoidance of the present moment, and gradually we want to come to terms with the possibility that living in the present might actually be something we want to encourage.

I have often met immigrants who have kept fond memories of their countries of origin, even though they would never think of returning there to live. Sometimes this fondness takes the form of "If only you could see how important I was back in my village . . ." This form of backward living is really quite sad, because it indicates a belief on the part of the person making the statement that he (or she) was only "real" or "authentic" there or then, but not here or now.

Nostalgia is another form of this backward living which can sometimes get people into trouble. Sometimes the whole human race seems to look back at a particular period of history as being a golden age of some sort. Not uncommonly, it is a religious belief of one sort or another that encourages this view. However, no matter how attractive the past looks, it is not possible to live in the past just by wishing it so.

This system would be fine, though distinctly inauthentic, if it were not for the fact that we can only actually live in the present moment. It is very important to come to terms with this fact. Otherwise life will actually be lived at a secondhand level in which nothing is real, everything is imagination or memory, and we are forced to create our own reality. This is the one tendency which must be avoided at all costs. Step One means being realistic, and beginning to come to terms with God's reality. In that reality, there are two things that are always true:

1. We can only make decisions in the present moment, and
2. We can only encounter God in the present moment.

THE COURSE OF RECOVERY IS BEAUTIFUL in its simplicity, dazzlingly complex in its execution. The alcoholic looks at his life, and admits that it is in a mess. He starts toward a path of belief which (at the very least) considers that there might be a power outside his own control that can give him back what his sickness has stolen from him, and then in one desperate gesture hurls the rotten remnants of his life in God's direction, and asks Him to do with them as He pleases. It is the desperation itself that becomes the prayer. It is the brokenness that brings the recovery.

In the medieval theology of the West, the same sort of paradox was explored, this time in relation to the sin of Adam. *O felix culpa*—O happy fault: "Had the apple not been taken, then Mary could not have become heaven's queen." This type of paradox is not that uncommon in religious experience, and certainly lies at the heart of the experience of the alcoholic. It is not uncommon to hear people at AA meetings hinting that they are glad, at a certain level, that they are alcoholics, because this knowledge not only allows them to make sense of a universe which until then was making no sense at all, but it also gives them a sense of personhood which was completely lacking before.

Chapter 6

The Twelve Steps
and the Life of the Church

THE REMAINING CHAPTERS OF THIS BOOK will examine the Twelve Steps themselves, commenting principally on similarities of experience with elements in the life of the Orthodox Church. Orthodox Christians are heirs of an extremely rich spiritual tradition. Limited neither by time nor by space, each person is a spiritual heir to every saint of every age. Holy Scripture, the books containing the liturgical texts, the writings of the Fathers of the Church—these are all the spiritual inheritance, worthy of a great deal of attention and effort. The literature is vast, and the wisdom very profound, even if it is also somewhat intimidating at times.

The Twelve Steps of AA outline a plan of action that defines a process of recovery from addiction—that is certain, and borne out by evidence. However, the Twelve Steps may also have some value in outlining, in a more general fashion, a way of repentance, of *metanoia*—the repentance preached by the Forerunner and by Christ Himself as being the necessary prelude to acceptance of the Kingdom. Indeed, there is a strong case for considering that the word *metanoia* in Christian theology and the word "recovery" in the vocabulary of AA have very similar meanings, even though their original goals are quite different and distinct.

Let us start by seeing what the life of the Church has to teach us about the nature of repentance and how an ongoing process of repentance brings us closer to God.

In the course of the year, the Church sets aside times of rejoicing and times of fasting. In practice, it is during the times of fasting[7]

---

7 There are four major periods of fasting in the Orthodox Church year: before the Feast of the Apostles, before the Feast of the Dormition, before Christmas, and the Great Fast before Easter.

that we feel most encouraged to follow the path of repentance, even though repentance can take place at any time. Of the periods of fasting, the Great Fast[8] before Pascha stands as supreme. This fast is preceded by a period of preparation that lasts three weeks, during which some of the most powerful examples of repentance in the Holy Gospels are placed before us, including the prodigal son and the publican in the Temple. The Sunday Gospels of Great Lent then continue these thoughts, providing powerful and important examples of repentance in action. The liturgical book that governs the prayer life of the Church during the whole period, called the Lenten Triodion,[8] is itself a treasure-house of spiritual guidance, giving dimension and focus to our thoughts about repentance and, in the way of Orthodox hymnody, weaving a beautiful tapestry of ideas and actions, examples and exhortations, all of them based on examples from the Gospels and other parts of Holy Scripture.

According to tradition, on the day we start to use the Triodion, the Sunday of the Publican and the Pharisee, the chanter finds the book resting beneath the icon of Christ on the icon screen in front of the altar. He receives the book as from the Person of Jesus Himself. The following morning, during the Orthros service, the chanter sings the words that will accompany our spiritual life during the ten weeks leading up to the celebration of Easter: "Open to me the doors of repentance, Giver of life."

This plea sets the tone for the whole of the next ten weeks: We ask God to open the door, so that our journey can begin. Repentance is not a destination; repentance is a journey, and a journey has to start somewhere. This particular journey starts here, at the door, three weeks before the start of Lent. With this prayer, each member of the Church is invited to consider himself standing at the beginning of Lent looking ahead at the path of repentance. For those who are fortunate enough to devote the following ten weeks to the full observation of the Church's prayers, that path is obvious,

---

8 *The Lenten Triodion*, translated from the original Greek by Mother Mary and Archimandrite Kallistos Ware, St. Tikkon's Seminary Press, South Canaan PA, 1994

and although challenging, it is available to all and well-trodden by the saints of every age. Along the path, prayer, fasting, and almsgiving are punctuated by the immediate interventions of God in the holy Sacraments, particularly in confession, anointing, and in Holy Communion, providing each person with the needed support and encouragement to continue.

The Lenten journey of repentance starts with an awareness that change is necessary, and ends with the transformation that outshines all transformations: the Resurrection of Our Lord and God and Savior, Jesus Christ.

It is likely that for most people, the fullest experience of Great Lent will take place in a monastery. In a monastery there is no need to think about what to eat or what to avoid eating, when to go to Church and when to stay in one's room, when to sleep and when to keep vigil. Such things are taken care of automatically, relieving the monks and the nuns (and any visitors who happen to be staying in the monastery) of the need to concern themselves with the details of life. Indeed, one of the most important aspects of monastic life is that it provides a safe environment in which to do the work each individual must do to tread the path toward salvation. Those who live in monasteries are greatly blessed to have the time and the means to follow, with little or no modification, the traditions of the Church in their fullest expression, outlined in Holy Scripture, the Lenten Triodion, and the classic Lenten text (often read in the refectory during Lent), the *Ladder of Divine Ascent* by Saint John Climakos.

For those neither living in a monastery, nor attending a parish church that provides a full liturgical expression of the Lenten Triodion—or indeed for those who do not have the luxury of being able to attend church on a frequent basis—the Twelve Steps may provide another outline, another choice, for embarking on the path of repentance. In their brevity, the Steps provide a straightforward way of following the path, but unlike the Lenten Triodion, they are not limited to any specific time, or any special set of circumstances.

Because of the way the Steps are written, they are able to enliven and restore the faith of many people, yet without influencing that faith directly. They are concerned with the background to faith—not with faith itself. It is for this reason that they do indeed resonate deeply with the life of the Orthodox Christian. They do the same thing for people of other faiths as well. From the beginning, use of the Steps transcended the normal boundaries of society, particularly religious boundaries. Protestant and Catholic alcoholics were able to use them and found, from the very start, that they were able to do so without compromising their own, or each other's, religious traditions.

It is said that Americans have a genius for practicality; if that is indeed the case, then the Twelve Steps may be viewed as an American contribution to the "path of repentance," available for those who want to use them to enliven and deepen their own spiritual experience. Like the thirty rungs in the plan of the *Ladder of Divine Ascent*, the Twelve Steps present a vision of repentance, a guidebook of transformation. Also like the Ladder, they are concerned with actual tasks that lead a person to a deeper and more lasting awareness of God. Unlike the Ladder of St. John, the Twelve Steps are not for monastic specialists, and although they were written down by a man of unquestioned ability, few would describe Bill W. as a spiritual giant. The Ladder was written by a monk (and a very holy monk at that) for monks, and although the wisdom of its words can certainly be adapted for use by people living in the world, its directives are sometimes difficult to apply outside the monastery.

The Twelve Steps require no experts. These Steps were initially taken by people broken by addiction, who were only just beginning to come to terms with many of the complexities of their own lives. In the course of completing them, they came on one element of certainty: If they invited God to help them in their alcoholism, He would do so. The Twelve Steps need no specialized knowledge, and they demand nothing except the willingness of the person who intends to use them. They can be modified to cope with any crisis or none, and they can be used in a wide variety of circumstances. Certainly they were designed for use in a particular context, but are applicable in most situations in the modern world. The Steps can and may be used by anyone.

The Twelve Steps state or suggest nothing that is not already a part of the life of the Church, and the person using them does not thereby become less Orthodox, or less Catholic, or less anything else. What the Steps do is to make a particular path of repentance obvious—providing a list of consecutive tasks which can be considered, and then put into practice or ignored, as the individual sees fit.

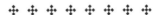

NEXT IT IS NECESSARY TO DISCOVER what a "path of repentance" actually means. The English word "repentance" has a rather sorry history. Although it is often used to translate the Greek word *metanoia*, it carries some negative connotations that the Greek word does not, including mental images of people wallowing in the guilt and self-torment that seem to be favored by certain Western writers. The Greek word, on the other hand, is a very positive one, and denotes a progressive and positive change of attitude on the part of the person concerned. It implies a change of mind, or a change of outlook, and its impetus is entirely forward-looking. In this sense, repentance may (but need not) include the dimension of sadness over past sins, but when it does so, it is in the context of reforming one's outlook in order to avoid making the same mistakes again in the future. Taking steps in a different direction, seeing the world with new eyes, starting over . . . these are the important features of repentance.

The theme of repentance is of utmost importance to a full understanding of the life of an Orthodox Christian. To compress a great deal of theology into a very few words, the heart of the Orthodox Christian experience of God consists in the transformation of the human condition which starts with repentance and ends in theosis.

Theosis, the transformation of the individual person into the closest possible union with God, is likely to occur towards the final stages of the spiritual journey. Repentance, on the other hand, is not only the initial stage of the spiritual journey, but also the path itself. It is in the development of a way of repentance that most of us have the most to learn, and about which the Church has the most to say. Repentance is a constant theme in the services of the Church, in Holy Scripture, and in the teachings and discussions of patristic authors. It is the first word of the Forerunner's message, and the last earthly act of the thief hanging on the cross beside the Savior. Repentance is the summary of prayer and sacrament, the act in which all human beings are beginners, all are equal.

Since everything we have and everything we are is a gift from God, repentance is one of the few genuine offerings that a person can make. Each person is free to make an offering of repentance to God, and in return He agrees to participate in the transformation of that person.

It hardly needs to be said that in repentance it is the aim to change *oneself*, not to change the rest of the world or to change the mind of God. In the Twelve Steps there is an implicit awareness that in any given situation in which there is a need for change, the person attempts to solve the problem by changing himself, not the rest of the world. It is not possible to repent on behalf of another person. Naturally, this makes the process very different from the expected behavior of individuals or groups of individuals (up to and including entire nations) that tend to set about solving problems by changing the rest of the world first. This distinction may mark one of the most important features of Twelve-Step living.

It is God, not the individual, who is in charge. It is the individual, not God, who needs to change.

ORTHODOX THEOLOGY HAS ALWAYS STRESSED that there is a very strong link between the person and the human body. The Church believes in the resurrection of the body, not the immortality of the soul. Rejecting the basic Platonic supposition that *real* reality can only ever be spiritual, and that the sort of reality that we can touch is both second-class and less than perfect, the Church has always asserted that God is the creator of heaven and earth, of what we can see and what we cannot see. Christian theology is adamant that it is not a secondary deity (a "demiurge," as taught by the Neoplatonists), but the Word of God Himself who is the agent of creation. Nevertheless, there is a persistent, recurring theme, particularly in some ascetic theology, that the soul is created by God, and that the body holds some sort of secondary place, and is in some senses alien to spiritual life. Sometimes when this tendency grows, it turns into a dualism in which the forces of evil and good are locked in an eternal conflict, with humanity caught in between the two. At other times it appears in the guise of Puritanism, in which there is a tendency to separate God from all but the most refined expressions of human existence. Naturally, such a doctrine tends to place the real world, and everything in it, under suspicion. It becomes easy to assume that certain elements of human existence are removed from God's influence, as if He created parts of the human being, but not all of it.

The whole theme of alcoholism and its treatment by spiritual means places this particular way of looking at things under a particularly strong light. What the program of AA maintains with some clarity is that God is not only able but also willing to plumb the depths of human experience and rescue individuals from the ravages of the disease. This places the thinking of AA solidly within the ranks of traditional theology in this respect, proclaiming that physical and spiritual health are very closely connected, and that God participates in the life of human beings even at levels where His presence might be unexpected.

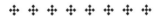

NOTHING IN THE TWELVE STEPS should actually take the place of any part of the normal life of an Orthodox Christian. Step Five, for example, is not the same as confession; Step Three is not the same as baptism. For the Orthodox Christian, the value of the Steps lies in the fact that they deal with themes and ideas which complement the life of the Church, rather than replacing it. The Steps are not compulsory in any sense of the word, and no one is forced to take them. Indeed, should anyone be forced to do them, the outcome would be less than desired.

At one level, a person "does" the Steps simply by reading them through. At a much deeper level, they can provide a lifetime of activity and spiritual progress. Each person is free to choose exactly at what level he or she wants to use them. Some people will go through them once; others will want to do so again and again. Some people find that as they pay attention to specific parts of their lives they want to change, it is good to do the Steps once more, focusing sharply on that aspect of their past lives. Others may manage to combine everything about them in one attempt.

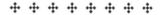

If anyone is using the Steps for a spiritual tune-up (as opposed to doing them to stay alive), there are several things that he or she might want to consider.

The Steps themselves do not mention sponsorship, but it is a factor that Orthodox Christians might like to take into account if they start to do the Steps. The figure of the sponsor is hinted at in Step Five, in which the individual is instructed to share his moral inventory with God and another human being, in the process of admitting the exact nature of his wrongs to himself. In practice, members of Twelve Step fellowships are often encouraged to turn to a clergyman at this point. In actual fact, it is not necessary for the person hearing a Fifth Step to be particularly well-trained, nor is it important that that person respond in any particular way, except, perhaps, to give some encouragement to the person doing the Step.

For most Orthodox, there always exists the possibility of asking a priest to be one's sponsor, although this is not essential. There is no sacramental nature to the sort of confession contained in the Steps, but there is also no reason why Step Five cannot become confession in the sacramental sense, or sacramental confession be made at the same time as doing the Fifth Step.

On the other hand, a person may want to choose to have a sponsor who has some knowledge of the Steps, rather than choosing a priest who may not know what they are all about. After all, some priests are likely to be suspicious of the Twelve Steps, particularly if they have little or no knowledge about recovery from addiction.

As with most spiritual relationships for lay people in the Orthodox Church, the Twelve Step sponsor and the one being sponsored have a great sense of freedom. The relationship may be terminated by either person at any time, although one might expect the sponsor to have a sense of spiritual responsibility, much as the spiritual father does in the Church. For the spiritual child, however, there is almost limitless freedom, since he (or she) is able to terminate the relationship at any time.

For monks and nuns, the situation is a little different. On deciding to enter a monastery, the novice is assigned a spiritual father or mother, and it is the job of that person to help the new candidate at every level to enter into the traditions and values of monastic life. Such a person need not necessarily be a priest, even in a monastery for men, but he should be someone who is deeply committed to the life of the monastery, and well-versed in bringing a novice to the fullness of the monastic experience.

Outside the monastery, the role of the parish priest is quite different from that of the monastic spiritual father. The priest is ordained, and his authority as a priest is not based on a voluntary agreement—his parishioners are expected to accept him as the parish priest, even though they need not choose to have him as a spiritual father. In fact, spiritual fathers are rather few in number, particularly outside Orthodox countries, and the status of the spiritual father is almost entirely charismatic in nature. A person (priest or layperson) is a spiritual father if his spiritual children say that he is. In fact, the title of spiritual father is seldom applied by a priest or a bishop to himself, and the best ones may categorically deny that they are capable of fulfilling that role at all.

There may be problems if a priest (particularly a young priest) tries to be a *de facto* spiritual father within his own parish and even outside it, giving advice on all and sundry. Within the monastery, and sometimes outside it, a spiritual father receives the grace of God to know his spiritual children at a level that is not always possible for the parish priest or the bishop. The parish ministry is of a slightly different order; wishing that it were otherwise—particularly wishing that parishes might become quasi-monasteries—is largely fruitless in situations where people are not able to exercise their ability to choose alternatives.

The spiritual father hears not only the sins of his spiritual children, but often also their thoughts. This is a very important factor in their spiritual growth. By the time someone does something sinful, the deed will have already been firmly associated in that person's thoughts. The corresponding process in AA is called "stinking thinking."

In its finest expression, there is a great deal of similarity between a spiritual father (or mother) and an AA sponsor. In AA the sponsor is generally someone who has a solid and vibrant sobriety, who knows and understands not only how the program works, but how to deal with the problems that occur along the way. The sponsor is someone who knows the problems "from the inside" and can help others follow the path he has already taken. Rarely will a sponsor be in a position to give advice unless it is specifically asked for, and then it will generally be given in the form of a choice. He (or she) will never try to take on responsibility for the person being sponsored, because it is an important part of that relationship to ensure that the person being sponsored should assume and administer responsibility for his own life.

Finally, on the topic of sponsors and spiritual directors, the Twelve Steps may provide a temporary spiritual program for anyone who is in the process of seeking a spiritual director, since the wording of the Steps allows them to be used by one person for his or her own benefit. However, it should be remembered that, for the recovering alcoholic, the context of the Steps is always social, and attendance at group meetings is more or less compulsory. Even recovering alcoholics in extremely isolated parts of the world will do their best to be in touch with others. With the advent of the internet and cell phones, it is possible for anyone to be in touch with almost anyone else in the world, given the desire and perhaps a sense of purpose. Under modern conditions there is always the possibility of having a meeting on the Internet, and sites of meetings can be found quite easily. Individuals using the Steps might benefit considerably from being in touch with others who are also doing the Steps.

THE MAIN DIFFICULTY in taking on the Twelve Steps is that they are not easy. The path requires diligence, honesty, and letting down a number of our defense systems usually kept in place to make sure we feel safe. Admitting that we can be wrong, even in principle, is very difficult for a lot of people. However, it is part of the spiritual repertoire of any Orthodox Christian who makes use of the sacrament of confession. Going to those whom we have wronged and making amends is also the practice of many Orthodox Christians who seek the forgiveness of those around them before they approach the Chalice for Holy Communion.

✤ ✤ ✤ ✤ ✤ ✤ ✤ ✤

IF YOU HAVE DECIDED TO USE THE TWELVE STEPS, it is suggested that you do them in order, and that you bring each one to some sort of finality before going on to the next.

Read each Step, looking at its original wording a number of times, asking yourself what it suggests to you. Does it look easy or difficult? Is it something you would like to do, or something that you would only do out of duty, or only if you thought it could really help you appreciate life more? Do you think it will be helpful to your understanding of your faith?

If you have vague feelings of discomfort at reading any one of the Steps, the likelihood is that that Step in particular is important to your spiritual growth.

Remember, do not try to do the Steps perfectly; just do each one as well as you can. As you are doing each Step, you will get an awareness of what you have to do to complete it—at least for the time being. In some ways the action Steps (which in themselves look rather difficult to do) are easier to complete than some of the others that are more theoretical in nature. However, it is beneficial to take each Step as it is, and to complete it as well as you can.

Part 2

The Twelve Steps

"But when he came to himself, he said, 'How many of my father's hired servants have bread and enough to spare, and I perish with hunger! I will arise and go to my father, and will say to him, "Father, I have sinned against heaven and before you, and I am no longer worthy to be called your son. Make me like one of your hired servants." ' And he arose and came to his father. But when he was a great way off, his father saw him and had compassion, and ran and fell on his neck and kissed him. . . . [And his father said,] "This my son was dead and is alive again; he was lost and is found."—Luke 15:17–20, 24

Chapter 7

Out of the Depths

Step 1. We admitted we were powerless [over alcohol] —that our lives had become unmanageable.

For I know that in me (that is, in my flesh) nothing good dwells; for to will is present with me, but how to perform what is good I do not find. For the good that I will to do, I do not do; but the evil I will not to do, that I practice. (Romans 7:18, 19)

I am a worm, and no man; / A reproach of men, and despised by the people. (Psalm 22:6)

"Eloi, Eloi, lama sabachthani?" which is translated, "My God, My God, why have You forsaken Me?" (Mark 15:34)

Significance for an Addicted Person
"First of all, we had to quit playing God."
(*Alcoholics Anonymous*, p. 62).

Each of the Steps assigns a specific task—definite, and sometimes very difficult. However, the wording of the Steps is usually gentle, in rather muted language. The words must not scare off the person who needs to follow this path. Far from being Twelve Commandments, the Steps simply describe a set of actions taken by one hundred anonymous people as they began to recover from alcoholism. The invitation to follow in their footsteps is implied, but not spoken. These are the suggested Steps of recovery, and they invite the individual to follow the path.

The words of the First Step form a very distinctive beginning. The idea of starting any task by admitting some sort of weakness—

or even defeat—does not sound at all promising. The normal way of going about most actions would be to gather one's strengths. So, right from the beginning of most human endeavors, the attitude of the person is adversarial—something to do with imposing one's will and one's views on someone or something else.

The pattern of the Steps is quite different. It starts with a notion of powerlessness. This is not the powerlessness of the defeatist, however. There is no defeat here. Rather, the road to success here starts with the notion that we can do nothing.

The word "unmanageable" is a very potent word. It represents a failed attempt to get on top of things. To "manage" is to control, and the image of a person controlling his or her own destiny is exactly the opposite of what we are about to attempt here. God is in control of the universe, and rightly so. However, He chooses to allow His control to be limited by the human will. Even the littlest human being can thwart the control of God by doing nothing more than thinking about it. As we shall see, the greatest offering a person can make to God is to surrender that power, and this is to allow God to be God once more. But this is jumping ahead to Steps along the path.

This is an important element in changing the way things might work in the life of a particular individual. As we notice from all sorts of examples in different walks of life, almost every idea, every project, every problem can be looked at in a variety of ways. However, our habitual practice is to approach a particular problem in the same way, time and time again, even when we know that it does not work very well.

The opportunity provided by the First Step is to lay aside known, tried, and (usually) failed ways of looking at things, and adopt the willingness to try something completely different.

If the First Step were the only Step, it would be a disaster. However, when the First Step is the prelude to the other Steps, it means that the person doing them is willing to break the cycle of previous behavior—to start on a path in which he or she is not going to impose a ready-made set of thoughts or ideas on the outcome. This is the same as saying that the person becomes willing to allow the course of events to develop in ways which he or she might find unexpected, or even unwanted.

- Taking the First Step means that we have tried other ways and they have not worked, and at last we are prepared to acknowledge that fact.
- Taking the First Step means we are at the end of our rope, and have no sense of being able to solve our problems by our own efforts.
- Taking the First Step only needs to be an awareness that there is something wrong with the world as we know it. That is all that is required, although not all that is possible.
- Taking the First Step means reality is grasped as it is, not as we would like it to be. There is probably a lot that could be said about how we create our own reality; what is important here is that the part of us which we identify as the "will"—the constant bottomless pit of desire—is not what is going to be relied on to make things good.

The purpose of the First Step is for the individual to be prepared to come to terms with the realization that the world which he understands may be nothing more than a false image, based on denial or some other form of deceit.

The Steps are careful not to encourage any sense of guilt, which is another route the individual can take to deflect the reality of the present moment. Guilt is a theme that will be examined in a number of different ways in the course of the Twelve Steps. However, at Step One there is no sense of "I have made some terrible errors, and I am now paying for it." Being powerless and finding one's life unmanageable are, on the contrary, free of such judgment, and this lack of judgment (or more especially, of condemnation) is a keynote of the Steps.

It is important to see how *little* is required at the beginning.

Step One happens as a reaction to hitting rock bottom, to experiencing that defining event which forces us to throw in the sponge, and give up the fight. Ironically, by refusing to fight any longer we become ready to start on the path to recovery.

At this point it is far too early to replace this false worldview with another. By the time that question has to be answered, the person will have a completely different (and in some senses, much more enlightened) view of what it means to have a worldview.

Many people defend their worldview because it gives them a sense of status, influence, or dignity. These are things we all crave, most of the time. Rarely, if ever, does a person willingly give up these sources of security, for to do so means to face the world in an undefended state.

The First Step implies that a person is at least prepared to consider that leaving behind the props of personal influence—so often based on a mistake or a deceit—is a possibility. It is thus a tremendously liberating Step, even though it also feels very dangerous. It is the awareness that the whole internal structure of a human personality might have to be ripped out and started again from the very beginning. Any behavior that insulates the individual from reality might have to go.

There is a certain truth to the fact that we create our reality on a daily basis. There is also a sense in which there is a definite reality outside our own experience with which we have to come to terms in one way or another. Somewhere in the middle of these two seemingly contradictory statements is a level of living and understanding that allows us to be free from the deceit of our own making, and free from the delusion that isolates us from the rest of the world.

The First Step makes sure that we are starting, that we are starting at the beginning, and that we make that beginning by facing the reality God has provided for us. This is true under all circumstances, even when we do not like what we see, and even if this is the first time we have ever done such a thing. It is time to let all defenses down—at least, before God.

Alcoholics and other addicts are not very good at looking reality straight in the face. To a certain extent, the same might be true of the whole human race. We compromise, tilt, color, and adorn reality with all sorts of devices aimed at making our lives feel more comfortable. Sometimes we indulge in outright distortion.

All that is required at the First Step—and it really is not difficult until you go back later to think about it—is a certain awareness that the person doing the Step is prepared to look at life on life's terms instead of his or her own terms. The opposite of this willingness is called "denial," and that involves any attempt to bend or twist the reality of one's own life in order to make the present moment more comfortable.

The reason denial is bad most of the time is that it encourages us to play the role of God in our lives. As we shall see, this is perhaps the very heart of the problem of understanding addiction and addictive behaviors, although it may not be very obvious here at the First Step. It is important to be aware that if we create our own reality we are in danger of missing out on some of the best things going, since inevitably God's reality will be preferable to our own.

In the course of the Steps, the sentiment, "I am God in my own life," is gradually going to be replaced with, "God is God in my life." To achieve that transformation, we need to start with an awareness that we cannot, in fact, manage our own lives: we are powerless over life, no matter how much we might protest that idea. By using drugs, or adopting behaviors whose main object is to change the way we feel (and often to make us stop feeling altogether), we start to create our own world, and that puts us, as it were, in the driving seat, and displaces God. God lets us do such a thing because He gives us the freedom to do such a thing. In giving us freedom, He takes a risk.

The claim, "I want to be God," looks preposterous in cold print, but yet that is exactly what is going on whenever we take over God's task of creating reality and replace it with a reality of our own.

SLOWLY, DURING THE COURSE OF THE STEPS, denial will be replaced with acceptance. Happily, at this early stage, it is enough simply to come to terms with the fact that there might be one or more forms of denial in one's life, and that things may not, in fact, be as they seem; later on it may become important to do something about it. Beliefs of all sorts—beliefs about oneself, one's capabilities, one's shortcomings—these will all need to be examined carefully before too long. For the time being, though, it is simply necessary to be aware that there is some work to be done.

FEELINGS ARE GREAT MOTIVATORS, but are not very good at telling us what to do. If they dominate our actions, we tend to get into a great deal of trouble. Fear, anger, despair, jealousy, and pride are all emotions that can play a very destructive role in our lives, but without them we may never be motivated to make any necessary changes in our life. Trying to push emotions away from us (even the negative emotions) is not the answer. In the course of the Twelve Steps it will become plain that it is possible to integrate all of our feelings into the spiritual path.

The purpose of Step One is to carry the alcoholic over the difficult threshold of starting something. The natural state of most alcoholics is to be drunk, lying on the floor, oblivious to everything. This state is interrupted (or perhaps punctuated) by periods of anguish and torment, in a world which makes the alcoholic feel that he not only has nothing to offer, but is also totally insignificant. He counteracts that powerlessness with his ego, which expands to the point where it, and it alone, is the highest power in the universe.

The First Step for an Orthodox Christian

Everyone, or almost everyone, has a sense that life is not as it should be. Most people experience this sentiment through a general feeling of dissatisfaction with their own lives, or with society in general. Something needs to be improved. Life is not fair. The human race (or one or more persons in particular) needs to change, and then everything will be all right. Another variation on this feeling is that something needs to happen before real life can begin. Very often, this sentiment is justified along the lines of "I need to become famous [or handsome, or thin, or qualified . . .] and then my life will be real," or "then my life will start."

A common spiritual error along the same lines is to believe that one may be able to become a better person—anywhere but here, and any time but now. The prayer attributed to the young Saint Augustine of Hippo, "Lord, make me pure, but not yet," is something that almost everyone, at every level of society, has considered at some time in their lives—often daily.

The principal spiritual hero for the First Step (and Steps Two through Five as well) is the prodigal son. He appears in a story Our Lord told His disciples, which is read to us as one of the Gospels in preparation for the beginning of Great Lent. His story is familiar, yet deserves to be read and reread. Having received his inheritance from his father (while the father was still living), the prodigal son went off and spent it all. In the end, he was penniless, he was starving, and he was forced to take a job looking after pigs—a job which was the height of degradation for a Jew.

While sitting there, watching the pigs eating, the prodigal son realized that he actually wanted to eat the food the pigs were eating. This is the point where he "came to himself"—he "realized" the reality of his situation. At that moment he did Step One.

Zacchaeus the tax collector shows us another example, from one of the other Gospels read during the pre-Lenten period. Zacchaeus wanted to see Jesus, but found it was difficult because he was a short man. Although it was somewhat ridiculous for a man of his age and standing, he decided that in order to see Jesus, he would have to climb a tree. He did not hang around at the back of the crowd, pretending he could see over everybody's head. He climbed the tree. At that moment, he did Step One.

Step One is particularly rich in examples from the Gospels read during the Lenten period. This next example is perhaps the best of all: the paralyzed man. This is the man who was brought to Jesus by four other men. They were so determined to be successful in their mission that they actually managed to get the man on his stretcher up to the roof of the house where Jesus was, and made a hole in the roof big enough to let the man and his stretcher go through. Quite how the owner of the house responded to this action is not recorded.

However, for our purposes, it is the paralyzed man who is the center of our attention. He simply allows himself to be carried. It is possible that he had absolutely no choice in the matter. Nevertheless, by allowing himself to be carried, he completed Step One.

In all three cases, these Gospel accounts show how the actions of the three men eventually brought them face-to-face with God—the father of the prodigal son in the first story, and Jesus in the second and third stories. The pattern is simple: the individual becomes aware (Step One), makes a move in the direction of God (Step Two), and in the ensuing encounter with God he is changed irrevocably (Step Three).

THE INHABITANTS OF SOME OF THE TOWNS of Galilee rejected Jesus and pushed Him away. The Gospel implies that they pushed Jesus away not because they did not know Him, but because they knew Him too well. They thought they knew what they were doing. They were in denial that Jesus was worth knowing, let alone that He was the Son of God. They thought that they were in the right, but the subsequent experience of those who are Christians indicates that they were not. To accomplish what they needed to do, they would have had to dispense with everything they thought was true, everything they thought was right, all their notions of wisdom and goodness, in order to see the world with fresh eyes, and to see the place of Jesus within it. This would have been very, very hard to do, more or less impossible, unless they could have started with a sense of their own powerlessness. They didn't. They did what human beings do naturally, which is to start with a sense of their own rightness. As a race, we are much more likely to want to be right than to want to be good. However, the Gospels do not call us to be right, but to be righteous.

YEARS AGO, I WAS SENT TO LIVE on an island in the Aegean Sea. I could speak no Greek when I arrived, and six months later my Greek was fairly fluent. This transformation occurred mainly because there was no one on the island who could speak very much English, and so I had to learn Greek if I wanted to communicate at all. The process that I endured in those six months was very painful. It was much like having a nervous breakdown, because, in order to learn Greek, I had to dispense with every sense of what it meant to rely on my native language. An inner belief that (a) everyone secretly speaks and thinks in English, and that (b) I had to think in English in order to communicate, had to be dropped. Once I let go of that perceived reality, I was free to proceed and adopt Greek as a language which I could use. My sense of powerlessness led, eventually, to a greater degree of ability.

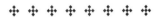

In the First Step, the individual is invited to put aside what is, after all, a natural notion of self-preservation in favor of realizing that he is, in fact, powerless. We have to leave behind the steam train in our minds that puffs, "I think I can, I think I can," in favor of a more accurate and useful realization that we have, in fact, no power whatsoever to improve our own lives, and that the more we try to do so, the worse we get. The reality, which is not difficult at all once we admit it, is that we have no power over people, places, and things. The fact that we feel that we ought to be all-powerful is not important. The fact that our educational system encourages us to think that that is what we need is also not important. In the school of the Lord's service, we have to start from a position of powerlessness, and the sooner we come to an awareness of that fact, the better.

Where we *are* powerful is in the area of making decisions for ourselves.

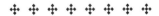

In the modern world, we are constantly being invited to take control of ourselves, our health, our bodies, our destinies, and our futures. "Control" is one of the most favored words of the people who run the advertising industry, because they know that it has universal appeal. It is difficult to get through an entire commercial break on the television without hearing the word "control," sometimes many times over.

We do not actually control very much; we just act as if we do. It is the path of the Steps to teach us that only God has control. Moreover, sometimes we will know what that control is, and sometimes we will not.

We are not attempting here to replace control with anarchy or passivity. What will, eventually, replace this false notion of control is a real and workable sense of cooperation between the human person and the will of God.

In the writings of the Fathers, the word "unmanageable" refers almost always to horses, an image which is somewhat distant from most of us today. However, the sense of "unbridled" is useful since it goes in the direction of what the alcoholic must feel, and must be aware of, if the First Step is going to be the turning point he so much desires.

For the Orthodox Christian, it may be fair to say that the most pressing aspect of Step One is reflected not so much in the chaotic unmanageability of life (although that is also there, even in the lives of the saints), but in a deep and terrible awareness of how far the person, and the life of the person, is from God. It is possible that a burning desire for God is associated with this powerless state, just as happens in the "realization" stage in the life of the prodigal son, just before he decides to return to his father. However, there is a danger. It may be at this stage that the burning desire itself is based on a vision of reality which belongs to one's unrecovered state, and that the vision of recovery is itself faulty. This was indeed true for the prodigal son, since the vision he had worked out for himself (i.e. to return home as a slave in his father's house) belonged to his own sick thinking, not to the vision of his father.

In practical terms it is important, in taking Step One, to realize just how far away one is from God, and how hopeless is the state of one's life when measured against any criteria, let alone when measured against the goodness of God. Nevertheless, the motives for taking the Step (the pain, the vision, the longing, the sense of hopelessness) might be based on a faulty vision. It is possible to start the Steps for entirely the wrong reasons, but so long as one is prepared to come to terms with that, there is no possibility of harm in the long run. The prodigal son was not capable of seeing his own motives in a clear light until after he had returned home, and his father had reinstated him. At that point he would have been able to go back and examine his motives and find them to be faulty. On the other hand, he may as likely have come to a realization that his motives did not, in the end, matter; what mattered was the fact *that* he took those first steps towards home, not *why* he took those steps.

Powerlessness feels very uncomfortable, and the more powerless we realize we are, the worse it feels. This is not a "feel-good" Step, since the purpose of it is to empty out any residual notion that we actually have any power within ourselves to help or heal ourselves. When we are dredging the bottom and realize that there is nothing there, we are starting to do this Step. We have to become childlike, totally dependent. We have to find an inner lack of strength. We have to be entirely dependent on forces and events that are outside our control. We have nothing to add, nothing to offer. The ground under our feet is not held up by our own power. The walls around us are not held by our own power. It is like waiting for the executioner to arrive, sitting in solitary confinement. Friendless, no contacts, no favors owed, no hope. It is lonely, and since we are totally vulnerable we are entirely afraid—fear pours out of our pores. This is reality, a reality that we try to hide, try to paper over. We try to convince ourselves: I am not that. But it is not true. There is no depth to which we could not sink, no wretchedness that we are not prepared to try.

The world's worst hangover, the hand of an arresting officer, a final tax demand, or the utter scorn of someone we love might trigger it. It may come to us at full force, or it may creep up on us. It may be a known fear, it may be unknown. But the certainty lies there, deep in the pain, deep in the awareness: we have sunk as deep as it is possible to go. All that can happen is that the waters flow to cover us up, and to wash us away, and cleanse the universe of our miserable selves. "I am a worm, and no man" (Psalm 22:6).

Every day of the year, with the exception of Bright Week, we read the Six Psalms[9] at the beginning of Orthros, the main morning service of the Church. These psalms are somewhat bewildering when read in our parishes, since generally very few people are present, and they are usually read at a time long after dawn. When read in a monastery at three-thirty or four o'clock in the morning, there is a greater sense of power in the words of these psalms. Those who study psychology often say that four in the morning is when people in the modern world experience their lowest emotional state in the twenty-four-hour period. Very often at that time our bodies are in rebellion, headaches and sleepiness almost more than we can bear, and our digestion in uproar. At this time we hear the words:

God, You *are* my God; early will I seek You; my soul thirsts for You; my flesh longs for You in a dry and thirsty land where there is no water. (Psalm 63:1)

and

Many are saying of me, there is no help for him in God. (Psalm 3:2)

Here we can feel sadness, loneliness, perhaps the beginnings of despair. The Church is saying to us that although these feelings are unpleasant, nevertheless, they have an authentic part to play in the total experience of prayer. Sometimes we are in deep depression, but that should not stop us from praying. Praying is not reserved just for the good times . . . or just for the bad times either.

It is the same with the First Step. It is uncomfortable, and it might make us feel depressed. However, like the Six Psalms, it is not the last word. Orthros, after all, ends with the Great Doxology. So also, there are eleven more Steps.

It is important to differentiate between a sense of great dissatisfaction with one's life and any thoughts which consist solely of

---

9 These are Psalms 3, 38, 63, 88, 103, and 143 according to the Hebrew numbering of the Psalms.

self-hatred or self-loathing. We are not at liberty to hate anything in God's creation, including ourselves. However, there is a certain sort of self-loathing which is actually quite useful—and that is self-loathing that urges us to action. Indeed, that is the whole point of "hitting bottom," since if, when you find your pain, you simply stay there for the rest of eternity, nothing beneficial has happened. However, if the details of the experience are severe enough to make sure that you actually go on to the other Steps, then the experience is not only something which will in the end be valued, but is actually something necessary.

Chapter 8

Lord, I Believe;
Help My Unbelief

Step 2: Came to believe that a Power greater than ourselves could restore us to sanity.

Seek the Lord while He may be found, / Call upon Him while He is near. (Isaiah 55:6)

Do not be afraid; only believe. (Mark 5:36)

[Jesus] asked His disciples, saying to them, "Who do men say that I am?" So they answered, "John the Baptist; but some say, Elijah; and others, one of the prophets." He said to them, "But who do you say that I am?" Peter answered and said to Him, "You are the Christ." (Mark 8:27b–29)

Significance for an Addicted Person

Step One is not unlike the incision a surgeon has to make before he is able to start the work he needs to do. It is painful and somewhat destructive, but it is absolutely necessary to achieve the required goal.

A person is led toward his own powerlessness, and then, perhaps for the first time ever, nothing happens to rescue him from this confrontation with reality. He has to stare at it, contemplate it, and so long as there is still a hint of resistance, he has to stay exactly where he is.

The moment he accepts it, he is ready to move on to the next Step. Once he has accepted his own powerlessness, there is an unspoken, yet important implication: There might be another option.

He is told, and slowly begins to recognize, that a power, any power, other than his own almighty ego is capable of helping him get back on track, helping him solve his dilemma.

His ego is not God. The ego of another human being is not God. Someone else is God.

And so the beautiful pilgrimage begins, and the desire for God is born. "As a hart longs for flowing streams, so longs my soul for Thee, O God. My soul thirsts for God, for the living God. When shall I come and behold the face of God?" (Psalm 42:1–2, RSV).

The rest of the Steps are a commentary on that pilgrimage.

It is tempting to suppose that alcohol is the king in the world of the individual alcoholic, and for some purposes that might be true. However, it is also true to say that it is the ego of the alcoholic, the broken or impaired ego, which is not only king, but also god.

This is why it is so important for the alcoholic to grasp, very near the beginning of his recovery, that there is a power outside himself which is greater than he is. Something, even in conceptual form, has to displace the broken ego which is playing god. At the beginning it matters little what that is. As recovery develops in the individual, it may be appropriate too for the idea of a Higher Power to become more and more closely identified with the Supreme Being of the universe, and indeed, as he enters the miraculous realms of recovery, he is more and more likely to want to make that connection. At the beginning, however, it is as well to strip down the idea of God, because otherwise all sorts of dangerous notions might be incorporated into the concept, and if that concept then grows roots it might not be capable of sustaining long-term sobriety. God can only be God if He is completely free of the alcoholic's ego.

Part of the recovery process for the alcoholic involves stripping down his vision of God, since his vision of God is flawed. The Second Step does not start with faith, but with a tentative, questioning attitude.

For the Orthodox Christian

When the prodigal son looks at the pig's food and realizes the despair of his situation, he does Step One. Almost immediately, he remembers his father, and he does Step Two.

There is a cartoon sometimes shown on television about a young chicken which has just been hatched, and yet (because this is a cartoon) she can talk. She wanders around the barnyard saying, in a small and pathetic voice, to anyone who will listen: "Are you my mommy?" The words are meant to bring tears to our eyes, because if this were a human situation, it would mean that the chicken had been abandoned by her mother, and that is one of the most basic fears a human being can imagine.

In the context of the Steps, we can see the same picture, but here the individual is a human person, and the question is, "Are you my God?"

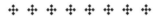

FOR THE ORTHODOX CHRISTIAN, particularly those fortunate to have been brought up in the faith, a great deal of the sacramental life of the Christian—baptism, chrismation, and Holy Communion—occurs before memories start. For them it was the faith of their parents and godparents that carried them into the church, just as the four men in the Gospel carried the paralyzed man into the presence of the Lord.

"Came to believe" could be the title for the story of any one of us. It implies, quite rightly, that belief is a journey, and not a destination.

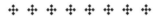

IN GROWING UP, ALMOST EVERYONE is able to make mistakes, and sometimes they are serious enough to affect our continued growth. St. Paul takes one aspect of this, and focuses on its implications: "When I was a child, I spoke as a child, I understood as a child, I thought as a child; but when I became a man, I put away childish things" (1 Corinthians 13:11).

In childhood we accumulate all sorts of ideas, thoughts, feelings, and phobias about all sorts of things. In particular, we adopt a wide variety of thoughts and experiences about God. We compare God with our parents, with our teachers, or with someone else whom we idolize. In most cases we are forced to make a comparison along the lines of "God must be something like my father, only more so"—or something similar.

With all the confusion of growing up—God, angels and saints, Santa Claus, the Easter bunny, the tooth fairy—it is quite likely that the image we have of God is also confused. This is particularly unfortunate in the case of Santa Claus—not the fourth-century Saint Nicholas, but the fellow that delivers gifts on Christmas Eve. First, as children we are encouraged to believe that he is real, and then (equally baffling) when we grow up a little we are encouraged to stop being childish, and to believe he does not exist.

In our thoughts, God may become something like an uncle, benevolent yet somewhat distant, and difficult to get hold of. Or he may become like a parent—the source of security, affection, sustenance, and shelter—but also the person most likely to punish us when we do wrong.

It is possible that God will end up in our minds as a sort of perfidious power who tantalizes and disappoints us in turns, or who takes delight in playing tricks on us. This can easily happen when this is also our experience of other people. We will always tend to project onto God the strengths, but also the failings, of those who are most important to us.

No matter what thoughts and ideas shape our notions of God, at some point in adult life it is necessary to do what Saint Paul says and to put aside the things of childhood, including whatever images and false icons of God exist from that childish world. We need to strip away the false, no matter how painful and sad it might be to watch it go.

A person who is brought up on an image of Jesus being "meek and mild" will not have an easy time dealing with abject tragedy in his life. His thoughts and feelings of God will fail him, since meekness and mildness offer very little in the event of a nuclear explosion or a plane crash or an unwanted pregnancy.

A person may come to the conclusion that God is someone to make bargains with, and that the whole purpose of existence is to get to the point where God has to do what that person wants. When that happens, he will be happy. Sadly, this is the path to addiction, and is the very opposite of what the Steps offer us.

In stripping away false or immature visions of God, there is a danger that the process will get too destructive. Sometimes we see this happening with the young people of the Church. They get to the point of destroying the old icons, but are not yet ready to take on God as He really is. Such people often leave the Church for a while. This may, indeed, be an important part of their spiritual development.

However, the important thing to bear in mind here is the goal of this work: for the Orthodox Christian, the Father is revealed to us through the life and teachings of the Son. The "power greater than ourselves" is ultimately always God the Father, shown to us by the Son, and experienced through the Holy Spirit.

This may look very complicated, until we come to realize that God's action in our lives does not, ultimately, depend on our mental image of Him. God is independent of our mental images, just as He is independent of our ego.

The traditional teaching of the Church helps us to get some clarification.

Through the Incarnation, the Second Person of the Holy Trinity became human. Thus we can be assured that as we deepen our relationship with God, we are going to be relating with someone who knows what it is to be a human being. The huge gulf that separates us from God is emptied of its threat. This means that the way we deal with God will, ultimately, be something like the way we deal with another person. God's love for us is of much the same order as our love for another human being, even though the intensity of that love may be far beyond what we can feel. Jesus Christ, the eternal Logos, shows us the Father by who He is and what He does. This is possible because we can fully know Jesus in His humanity, even though that humanity is a delight and a wonder beyond the more normal level of awareness we experience when dealing with each other in everyday life.

The theology of icons safeguards an awareness that while we may be intimate with God, we are not going to comprehend Him, we are not going to have power over Him or completely contain

Him within our minds. According to an ancient tradition of the Church, the Father remains beyond depiction, and cannot be shown in icons except in a very symbolic way. For our purposes, this implies that the Father can only ever be a power outside and greater than ourselves. In effect, the Father cannot be depicted on icons because He is beyond the painter's brush, totally unknowable except by His own choice, through revelation. The Son is quite different in this respect, because His humanity places Him in a vulnerable position. We can construct false notions of the Son of God—and do. There are, after all, "bad" icons in the brains of many of us.

In taking flesh, the Son of God went through a process called *kenosis* by the theologians—an emptying. In emptying Himself, He made Himself available to us—He placed Himself within our reach. We learn that we can approach God just as we approach another human being, and we are not going to be burned by the fierceness of His presence. We will not be consumed by His love, but gently warmed by His kindness.

In becoming human, Jesus took (and takes) a risk. He makes Himself vulnerable, because only thus are we able to enter into a relationship with Him. There is always an element of vulnerability in relationships. God makes Himself vulnerable for our sake.

The process of "coming to believe" involves making oneself vulnerable to God.

There is one example in the Gospels that indicates the sense of Step Two with great exactness. It is in the story of the father who brings his son to Jesus for healing. The boy is epileptic, and the man asks Jesus if He can do anything to help him. At this point Jesus takes the theme, and gives it right back to the man: it is the man's belief that will achieve the required change. The man takes the challenge, but hands it back to Jesus in this form: "I believe; help my unbelief!" (Mark 9:24).

Belief is not the reward of mental effort: it is a direct result of the relationship between a person and God. In some ways, it is a gift from God, given in return for the trust and confidence of the person. Put another way, we cannot make belief happen, just by willing it so. "Came to believe" is not the path of our effort; it is the path of accepting God's effort.

Taking Step Two is like a child jumping off a ledge and into the arms of his parent. The child contributes trust and innocence, and the parent provides security and capability and strength.

Taking Step Two is coming to an awareness that God is nearer and more concerned with every aspect of our lives than we previously thought.

WHEN I WAS IN MY TEEN YEARS, I adopted an aunt. She was very generous in spirit, and although I sometimes tried her patience, she was almost always kind and welcoming. Her husband, who had died before I met her, had been an alcoholic, and had joined AA in the very early days. It was actually because of her that I first heard of the existence of AA. She was a great collector of all sorts of things, including various pictures and plates she had accumulated during the course of her long and interesting life. She also had a great deal of faith, and she wasn't averse to talking about it, under the right circumstances, in a very straightforward way.

On the wall in the main living room there was a plate. I think it was late-eighteenth-century. It was cream-colored and in the center there was a quotation from Genesis: "Thou God Seest Me."

One day I was helping my aunt do some housework in that room. I was doing the vacuuming, and she was dusting. She got to the plate on the wall and turned to me and said: "When this plate was made, I think it was probably used to frighten children into behaving, since they knew that God was watching them. I don't see it that way at all," she said. "I think it means that God loves us so much, He cannot bear to take His eyes off us." She went on to dust something else, to think about something else, unaware of the impact of what she had just said. Such was my aunt. I miss her a lot.

WHEN THE PUBLICAN WENT INTO THE TEMPLE, we are not told whether or not he noticed the Pharisee, although we know that the Pharisee noticed him. In all likelihood, he did not, since the story says that the Publican would not even lift his eyes to heaven. The image of someone calling out to heaven in his heart, yet not looking upwards, is a clear image of someone taking Step Two.

The four men carrying the paralytic were not sure what they were doing until they actually deposited the man at Jesus' feet, and his healing (of both body and soul) took place before their eyes. While they were simply carrying the man toward the house, up the steps, and letting him down through the roof, they did not *know* that they would achieve anything—apart from the probability that they would make everyone angry, especially the owner of the house. As they walked toward the house, they were getting nearer and nearer the point where they would meet God, but they did not know it at the time. They were doing Step Two right then.

One of the most beautiful encounters in the Gospels takes place between Jesus and Peter on the occasion when Jesus walks on the water. Peter, sitting in the boat, shouts out into the darkness: " 'Lord, if it is You, command me to come to You on the water.' So He said, 'Come.' And when Peter had come down out of the boat, he walked on the water to go to Jesus. But when he saw that the wind *was* boisterous, he was afraid; and beginning to sink he cried out, saying, 'Lord, save me!' And immediately Jesus stretched out *His* hand and caught him" (Matthew 14:28–31).

Peter relies on Jesus when he initially climbs out of the boat, and again when Jesus catches him at the end of the story. It is only in the middle, when he realizes what he is doing, that he relies on his own abilities, and starts to sink.

Here we see the Apostle Peter doing Step Two.

Chapter 9

Surrendering to God

Step 3: Made a decision to turn our will and our lives over to the care of God as we understood Him.

Trust in the Lord with all your heart, / And lean not on your own understanding; / In all your ways acknowledge Him, / And He shall direct your paths. (Proverbs 3:5–6)

Do not seek what you should eat or what you should drink, nor have an anxious mind. For all these things the nations of the world seek after, and your Father knows that you need these things. But seek the kingdom of God, and all these things shall be added to you. (Luke 12:29–31)

"Father, 'into Your hands I commit My spirit.'" (Luke 23:46)

Significance for an Addicted Person

In the Big Book of Alcoholics Anonymous, the condition of the alcoholic is characterized as "self-will run riot." This self-will is expressed in a combination of stubbornness, irresponsibility, and the desire to control. Having been brought to his knees by his drinking, the alcoholic has no option but to turn over his life and will to a power beyond his own ego; his own ego is bankrupt.

This is perhaps the most difficult and the easiest thing that the recovering alcoholic will do in the course of his entire life. It is easy to do, and very difficult to do well.

This Step marks a tremendous transition for the person doing it. It marks the end of one way of life and the beginning of another. It demands a great deal of spiritual maturity from someone doing it for the first time, but as with some of the other Steps, the difficulty is only seen through the clear eyes of someone looking in retrospect, not through the bleary eyes of the person longing to be free from his pain.

In the Big Book, a special prayer—the first assigned to a particular Step—is suggested:

"God, I offer myself to Thee—to build with me and to do with me as Thou wilt. Relieve me of the bondage of self, that I may better do Thy will. Take away my difficulties, that victory over them may bear witness to those I would help of Thy Power, Thy Love, and Thy Way of life. May I do Thy will always!"

The first three Steps are the necessary beginning to the recovery process. They are absolutely crucial, and radically change the way a person thinks and interprets his feelings. This sort of change is rarely observed in any other context, with the possible exception of a major religious conversion.

Bill W. wrote that the first three Steps contain three pertinent ideas:

(a) That we were alcoholic and could not manage our own lives.

(b) That probably no human power could have relieved our alcoholism.

(c) That God could and would if He were sought.

Bill goes on to explain: "The first requirement is that we be convinced that any life run on self-will can hardly be a success. On that basis we are almost always in collision with something or somebody, even though our motives are good. Most people try to live by self-propulsion. Each person is like an actor who wants to run the whole show; is forever trying to arrange the lights, the ballet, the scenery and the rest of the players in his own way. If his arrangements would only stay put, if only people would do as he wished, the show would be great. Everybody, including himself, would be pleased. Life would be wonderful. In trying to make these arrangements our actor may sometimes be quite virtuous. He may be kind, considerate, patient, generous; even modest and self-sacrificing. On the other hand, he may be mean, egotistical, selfish and dishonest. But, as with most humans, he is more likely to have varied traits" (*Alcoholics Anonymous,* p. 60).

The First Step happens when a person comes to an awareness that he is powerless.

The Second Step consists in his putting out his hand, like a child seeking help and kindness, and finding that there is someone out there who will take it.

The Third Step is to surrender his ego (i.e. what he thinks he wants out of life) to that anonymous power, dressed however he thinks fit, in whatever terms, whether theologically precise or completely heretical. This is the final part of the jigsaw.

In the nonalcoholic world, this action might well look rash, because people may want to be sure of the credentials of the Higher Power they are handing their lives over to, before they do so. Very often, they may have preconditions about how such a power should behave, and how such a power should react. Here, however, there is a problem. If a person defines the Higher Power prior to surrendering his life and his will, then the Power is limited (even slightly) by his own imagination, his own thinking. The result is clearly a power much nearer the alcoholic's ego—it is a power that can be contained within the human imagination. This is not the Higher Power outside the person. This is the higher power within the person. This difference is crucial.

For the Orthodox Christian

In the full round of services, the Lord's Prayer is recited at least fifteen times a day, and during Great Lent many more times. It forms one of the spiritual high points of the Divine Liturgy, and exists for all of us as one of the most basic of spiritual guides, given to us by Our Lord Himself. In this prayer comes the phrase, "Thy will be done on earth as it is in heaven."

This is, essentially, the plea of Step Three: "Thy will be done!"

There is no more characteristic way of giving sovereignty to God, whether at a national, parish, or personal level. Jesus Himself, in showing us this path, declared that He came not to do His own will, but rather the will of His Father (John 6:36). When faced with the anguish of His Passion, the dreadful pain and suffering, He prayed explicitly that the will of His Father might be done.

The way in which we are able to do Step Three depends very much on the state of our spiritual health. Sometimes, particularly when we are feeling weak, it may be necessary to hand our lives and our will over to God many times in the course of an hour—sometimes in the course of a minute. At other times, it seems most natural to let God work in our lives. However, there needs to be a caveat here. Once we have done Step Three, it does not mean that everything that happens in our life from that moment on is the will of God. Our weakness is far stronger than that. In fact, it will almost never happen that we are certain of the will of God in any given situation. If we are certain, it almost always means that we have relieved God of our will and our life, and we are back in the driver's seat, this time imagining that we are automatically doing what God wants us to do. The good that we do in Step Three we do in trust, not in certainty.

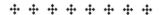

THE EPISTLE OF JAMES (4:7) encourages us to "submit yourselves . . . to God." This is necessary in small things as well as great, and under all and every condition in which the human person can find himself or herself.

The prodigal son does Step Three when he decides he will return to his father's house, admit that he was wrong, and ask his father to take him back as one of the hired servants. Naturally, part of his (and our) return home is to leave all the consequences of that return home to the father. It is the father, not the son, who decides the conditions of his return.

The act of surrender of Step Three is like diving off a cliff. There are no assurances, no guarantees; and no amount of wisdom and knowledge is going to be of any assistance. Even common sense is of no use. Indeed, common sense is one of the things that has to be put aside, because it implies that we should aim to be in control of our own lives.

The rich young man coming to Jesus is faced with the dilemma exactly when Jesus asks him to go and sell all that he has, and to give the proceeds to the poor, before embarking on his discipleship. The significance appears all the greater when one realizes that the young man was very wealthy. It is as if Jesus is demanding that the man give away—surrender—the very thing in his life that makes the most sense, that shows who he is as a person. It is the thing that allows him to function, to define himself and others, to "be" who he is. This is the quality—the wealth—which Jesus requires.

This is exactly the dilemma of the alcoholic. Whether he likes it or not (and most do not), alcohol defines the life of the drinking alcoholic. It makes sense of everything, the good and bad, and motivates his being. Giving it up is the most difficult task that could ever be asked of him, even when we can see it against the (poor) example of the rich young man.

For the nonalcoholic, it is not actually necessary to decide exactly what it is that God wants us to surrender. If we surrender our whole life, God will be able to take what He needs.

There are those, particularly those who have a deeply religious framework to their world, who feel it may indeed be dangerous to surrender in the way described here. What would happen, for example, if instead of surrendering to God, I actually surrendered myself into the power of Satan, or some other power of evil?

For Orthodox Christians, this should not present a real problem. After all, Jesus talking to His disciples makes the following comment: "If you then, being evil, know how to give good gifts to your children, how much more will your Father who is in heaven give good things to those who ask Him!" (Matthew 7:11). Moreover, the notion that the power of evil is able to thwart the power of God in some eternal way is utterly alien to Christian tradition. We are able to choose to do evil, to be sure, but the idea of surrendering one's will and one's life to God, only to find that in fact one has surrendered to Satan, is far removed from our understanding of God, and belongs only to those religious traditions in which good and evil are equally matched. Christianity is most certainly not such a religion.

AA members tend to become spiritually astute in sobriety, ever-vigilant in guarding their sobriety, and extending a helpful hand to those who need it. If there had ever been cases of people unknowingly falling into the ways of the evil one by taking Step Three, then most assuredly the collective membership of AA would know about it and talk about it openly. After all, it is an anonymous society, not a secret one. There is no record of such an event ever taking place.

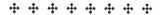

As already stated, life as an Orthodox Christian is about the transformation of the individual. This transformation starts with repentance and ends in theosis. It is true that sometimes it seems that we expend a great deal of energy keeping the best from the past; nevertheless, the thrust of the Orthodox faith is always forward, and in the direction of change and transformation.

The highest expression of our Church life occurs when the priest or deacon lifts the bread and the wine during the Divine Liturgy just after the words of Christ at the Last Supper have been recited. Here the words in Greek are so poignant, so full of meaning, that they almost defy a full understanding in any other language: *Ta Sa ek ton Son:* "We offer to You these things which are Your own, on behalf of all and through all."

The Epiclesis and the offering of the bread and wine at the Divine Liturgy constitute a peak experience of the Church, done at the command of our Lord, and performed with joy. The alcoholic doing Step Three for the first time may do so in a spirit of desperation. Nevertheless, there is a common element here: the act of "turning over." This is *the* offering, the *anaphora*, and offering involves the surrender of what is offered.

As illustrated so beautifully in the Divine Liturgy, our most authentic act of offering to God is accompanied by an awareness that God already has everything, and that everything we have comes from Him. The Third Step, which represents one of the highest mystical steps in the journey of recovery, involves offering back to God the one gift we actually have to give: our freedom, or our ability to make choices. We turn over "our life and our will" to God. That really does not leave anything. To us belongs the act of offering. How God will accept our offering is God's choice.

The sense that in Step Three we are returning to God what is already His, just as we do in the Divine Liturgy, is highlighted by the following exchange from the sixth century:

St. Barsanuphios was asked: "God created man free, and He Himself says: 'Without me you can do nothing' (John 15:5). I ask you, how can one reconcile freedom with the fact that without God one can do nothing?"

The Saint replied: "God created man free so that he might incline toward the good; but inclining toward it by his free will, he is in no condition to perform the good without the help of God, for it is written: 'It is not of him that willeth, nor of him that runneth, but of God that showeth mercy' (Romans 9:16). And so, when a man bends his heart toward the good, and calls on the help of God, then God, heeding his good fervor, will grant him strength for doing good."[10]

Here we see that calling on God results in God helping the person. Both the call to God (on the part of a free man) and the loving response of God are necessary.

✢ ✢ ✢ ✢ ✢ ✢ ✢ ✢

STEP THREE IS THE POINT where the individual is invited to dethrone his own ego and to put his entire life in God's care. From this point on, there is no certain knowledge of what might happen as a result; that is God's responsibility, not that of the person doing the Step.

This same reliance on God is reflected in the usage of Orthodox Christians who punctuate their speech with "if God wills" and "may it be blessed" when referring to some future plan.

After Step Three, all the outcomes of all our plans are in God's hand.

---

10 Saints Barsanuphius and John, *Guidance Toward Spiritual Life*, trans. Fr. Seraphim Rose, St. Herman of Alaska Brotherhood, 1990, p. 133

Chapter 10

The Doors of Repentance

Step 4. Made a searching and fearless moral inventory of ourselves.

Step 5. Admitted to God, to ourselves, and to another human being the exact nature of our wrongs.

> *First cleanse the inside of the cup and dish, that the outside of them may be clean also.* (Matthew 23:26)

> *Whatever you have spoken in the dark will be heard in the light, and what you have spoken in the ear in inner rooms will be proclaimed on the housetops.* (Luke 12:3)

> *Let each one examine his own work.* (Galatians 6:4)

This is the first occurrence of a pair of Steps in which the preparation of the first leads to the action of the second. In AA literature, the Steps are almost always treated separately. However, in the present book Step Four will be considered as preparation for, and combined with Step Five, Step Six with Step Seven, and Step Eight with Step Nine.

Significance for an Addicted Person

The alcoholic is very bad at seeing himself in a clear light. He is either the greatest hero of the hour, or the most miserable wretch on the face of the earth. Sometimes he is both at once.

In coming to a clear picture of who he is, the alcoholic has to take a good look at the person he has been. In most cases this will not be a particularly pretty picture, and his memories will not be happy ones. Nevertheless, in a straightforward, incisive way, Step Four allows him to dive right into the examination of who that person has been.

It is worth bearing in mind that this is Step Four, and not Step One. It is important to come to terms with one's own powerlessness, to seek God's help, then to surrender to God, *before* attempting Step Four. Otherwise, the Step will simply turn into a sort of self-condemnation.

Notice, though, that the Step does not state that we have to start thinking about the things that make us feel guilty. "Owning up" or "coming clean" would under most circumstances involve talking about things of which one was ashamed. Not so Step Four. Here we are invited to look at the complete picture: not just what we did wrong, what mistakes we made, or what did not go right. Here we are invited to look even at the roots of our errors, and according to AA's wisdom, the most dangerous root of all is resentment.

"Resentment is the 'number one' offender. It destroys more alcoholics than anything else. From it stem all forms of spiritual disease, for we have been not only mentally and physically ill, we have been spiritually sick" (*Alcoholics Anonymous*, p. 64).

Resentments are insidious little feelings. They are insidious because they are so small—so small that it is easy to overlook them. However, they are the perpetual fuel for the fire of wrongdoing and the motive behind almost everything that is wrong in our lives. Their main function is to cause us to do bad things. Their purpose is to fuel sin.

We start picking up resentments from the time we are born. By the time we can speak, we have resentments of all sorts.

The recovering person needs to ask himself: Of whom am I resentful and why? Bill W. says quite explicitly that if the alcoholic cannot answer that question satisfactorily, he will drink again. The nonalcoholic does not have such a threat hanging over him, but these words should certainly cause a person to take notice. Resentment is a spiritual killer.

The heart of the process of Step Four is to start making a list of people and situations against whom we hold resentments, then carefully to examine why we hold the resentments we do. As we start the list with obvious resentments, other, less obvious ones will generally occur to us.

In almost every case, there will be an element of our own wrong-doing attached to each resentment. Even though we generally feel resentment most strongly against the actions of others, it is important to see our own contribution, since it is there (and only there) that we can make a difference.

It matters little whether we still know these people or whether they belong to our ancient history. It matters little whether they have died or not—it is quite possible to hold a great resentment against a dead person. What is important is that resentments be rooted out and rendered harmless.

Next to resentment in importance comes fear. Fear is a catchall term, used to describe a number of different emotional states, most of which are destructive. Of these, the most surprising is often that fear is simply another form of anger, another word whose definition is rather wide.

There are three main areas of life where almost everyone has problems, at least some of the time. Money is often a cause of anguish, whether because of extravagance, or fear of monetary insecurity, or both. Almost everything to do with sex can be a problem, whether one is single or married. Eating habits and food in general is another source of great pain for many people. Thus, even without alcohol or other addictive substances to worry about, the nonaddict has plenty of these common areas of problems on which to concentrate, quite apart from things of a more idiosyncratic nature.

We are complicated men and women. Thoughts and feelings surge through our bodies almost all the time. Almost everything that is noble and true and good and lovely can also become shoddy and even disgraceful when it is used inappropriately. Getting on well with people is entirely laudable, but being a "people-pleaser" is far from the mark. Being a good parent is a difficult (if not impossible) task, but having an overdeveloped sense of responsibility for one's children is not helpful at all. Being a meddler in the affairs of others needs to be recognized, as does the massive and difficult theme of control. We were given places in this quasi-paradise to do all sorts of things, but to control it was not one of them. Humility is good; low self-esteem is not. Respect is good; fear of authority is not. Righteous indignation at some work of perfidy is praiseworthy; rage is not. We need to feel, but we must not let our feelings rule us. We need to be responsible, serious, and level-headed, yet God also seems to want us to have fun. We are, each one of us, sexual, and yet the expression of that sexuality is something about which we need to take very great care.

In all these areas, it is the degree, rather than the existence, of a particular element in our lives that is important. There is almost no room for black-and-white thinking here, since these are not things that either do, or do not, exist.

It is for this reason that Step Five follows Four. It is possible, even likely, that someone would make a tremendous mess of Step Four on his or her own. However, that mistake will last only until Step Five, when another human being is present to help the person doing the Steps to see things a little more clearly.

There are no obvious examples of people doing Step Four in the Bible, since the whole action of Step Four is private. Its public manifestation, however, has a large number of examples, as we shall see in the next section.

If there were ever a competition for the greatest sinner, only one person would win, and no one but God could be the referee of such an event. In a spiritual sense, however, it is valuable for each person to believe herself or himself to be the worst sinner ever—not because he cannot be forgiven, but because he can!

So, the alcoholic looks at his resentments, his mistakes, his faults, and his character flaws. He is instructed to be fearless— because leaving even a little resentment behind could be dangerous. Resentments, in particular, are like tiny sparks of fire that can, in the end, become a seething mass of destructive emotions. For the alcoholic, destructive emotion generally leads back to the one thing he is trying to escape: drinking.

There are many good guides and workbooks available to direct people through Step Four. One of the best I have seen is published by Overeaters Anonymous.[11] Another is in the relevant chapters of

11 *The Twelve-Step Workbook of Overeaters Anonymous,* Overeaters Anonymous, Torrance, CA, 1993

Dr. Patrick Carne's book, *A Gentle Path through the Twelve Steps.*[12]

Notice that at this point we are not seeking to do anything with the revelations we glean about ourselves. Here we are simply aware that they are there. The most common and effective way to get rid of resentments is to pray for those very people against whom we hold grudges. Even if, at the beginning, we have to pray for them through clenched teeth, that is at least a start. Once we have initiated that activity, we are also in a better situation to start learning to forgive ourselves for our own parts in the resentment-causing events. To attempt to forgive oneself without forgiving others is an impossibility.

Step Five: Admitted to God, to ourselves, and to another human being the exact nature of our wrongs.

> *Let us cast off the works of darkness.* (Romans 13:12)

> *Confess your trespasses to one another, and pray for one another, that you may be healed.* (James 5:16)

> *If we confess our sins, He is faithful and just to forgive us our sins and to cleanse us from all unrighteousness.* (1 John 1:9)

Significance for an Addicted Person

If there is one single thing that alcoholics are very bad at—whether they have been drinking or not—it has to be telling the truth about themselves. The entire condition of addiction is based largely on a lack of truth.

Although Step Four is not quite as explicit as Step Five, by the time we get here it is quite apparent that what we need to talk about are our wrongs. Put another way, things we have done wrong in the past are likely to hurt us in the present or in the future, whereas things we have done well probably will not. All the contrary emotions we have that thrive on guilt need to be taken out, given a good airing, and shaken down, before they can rightfully take their

---

12 *A Gentle Path through the Twelve Steps,* Patrick Carnes, Ph.D., Hazelden, Center City, MN, 1993

places in our repertoire of human interaction once more. We need to wipe the slate clean.

The wording of the Step is explicit in another sense, also. We are invited to share our wrongdoings with God (first), with ourselves (second), and with another human being. The stipulation is not explicit, but it is expected that the human being will be alive, awake, and in the same room when Step Five is taking place. It is no mistake that God comes first in the list. By the time the recovering person has done the first four Steps he will, more than likely, have reached the conclusion that God knows him better than he knows himself. There is very little point in pretending to God.

Admitting his past faults to himself is a novelty for the alcoholic, who, during the drinking days, was quite capable of stating that black was white and getting himself to believe it. A long-time friend of mine who is in AA talks of the fact that he used to write himself notes when he was drunk which said things like: "Everything is all right," or "Nothing bad happened." This was intended (he assumed) to give himself reassurance the following day when he tried to piece together the activities of the previous evening. Unfortunately, these notes actually had the opposite effect, because the next morning he naturally assumed that he had actually been attempting to play a trick *on himself*, and thus these notes, together with the endemic paranoia of the alcoholic, only made him feel worse, leaving him to wonder what he had actually done.

Admitting his faults to another human being is a sure sign that the alcoholic is in recovery. Once he realizes how easy it is to tell the truth (since there is no tangled web to create, remember, and coordinate), telling the truth brings a great sense of relief, no matter how unpleasant the details might be.

Certainly, by this point, the person in recovery is beginning to distance himself from his former "old" self, and the more he can tell truthful stories about just how bad his life had become, the more chance there is that he will have a speedy and long-lasting recovery.

Alcoholics are often cautioned that it is important that they include all their wrongdoings in this Step. The Step does not refer solely to wrongdoings committed while drinking. The idea is actually much more subtle than that. It is partly because a person has difficulty living with feelings of guilt and failure that drinking becomes such a friendly support in the first place. Removing the roots of the reasons a person drinks is a necessary part of the treatment, and Step Five is the place to make sure that happens. It is not the whole of the treatment, but it is an important part of it.

This is the first of the Steps which is a direct result of the previous Step. Preparation and action are divided here in a way which goes against the alcoholic's method of doing things. First he is asked to contemplate something, but take no action. Then he is asked to take action based on his contemplation. Most alcoholics do not find this easy; they generally prefer to do the action and the thinking at the same time, hoping that no one will notice that they are doing neither very well.

Almost everything an alcoholic says is adjusted somewhat, according to a complicated and highly personalized set of rules and standards. Half-truths, exaggeration, and hyperbole are just the beginning. If a drinking alcoholic says he is good in some way, he is usually trying to conceal some other, more important, fault. If he accuses himself of being bad, he usually does so with a view to gaining sympathy from his listener.

By the time he is ready to do his Fifth Step, however, he is beginning to come to terms with honesty and truth. It is helpful to him if he is encouraged to talk without making any mental adjustments. Gradually, he comes to acknowledge that life is as he finds it.

For the Orthodox Christian

Step Four looks very much like the sort of preparation one may make for confession. Under most circumstances, it is possible to combine Step Five with going to confession, or to use the same material twice, once in the context of the Steps with a lay sponsor, then again in the context of the Sacrament of Confession with a priest. "Inventory" is a rather modern word which suggests taking stock of one's life. "Moral inventory" places the activity within certain boundaries, and those boundaries are usually the areas where we need to confess, and where we need to receive God's forgiveness. It is worth bearing in mind that "moral inventory" is not necessarily limited to things that we have done wrong. Under most circumstances, it will also be a time for taking stock of exactly what is right with a particular life, in a way which confession rarely is.

The mistakes that people often make in confession, however, are exactly the same sort of mistakes that one should try to avoid in Steps Four and Five, if one is going to get the full benefit of doing the Steps.

Some people spend all their time in confession talking about the wrongs of others. This is often framed in such a way that the apparent sin (on the part of the speaker) is a feeling of anger at the actions of the person who is not present.

There are two points to watch for here. The first is that having a feeling is not, actually, a sin. Feeling angry, or feeling sad, or feeling happy are not sins: they are feelings. Certainly there is a gray area here, since we can sometimes encourage feelings (and in so doing sin may be involved), but we cannot really create them. They come and they go. Since we have very little authority over them (in this general sense), it is very difficult for feelings to be sinful, since a sin has to involve a sense that we want something bad to happen. Where we can sin, and quite easily too, is to act on a feeling—particularly a negative feeling. For example, if we are angry, and we act out that anger in the form of spitefulness, dishonesty, or in some other way, then we can certainly sin. Even if we plan to hurt someone because we are angry, we are already doing something wrong. However, the feeling of anger, on its own, is not a sin.

There is another point here. Sometimes in confession people are so busy justifying things they have done that they hardly manage to mention the things they have done wrong at all. In order to stop that from happening, it is quite appropriate to say at the beginning: "Here are the things I have done wrong since my last confession," then simply list events and situations in which you have done less well than you could have.

Confession, and Steps Four and Five, are not occasions when we need to show ourselves in our best light, nor is it a time to paint the blackest picture possible. The whole point of the exercise is to see ourselves with some clarity, neither exaggerating our bad points, nor trying to provide justification for our actions. It is, in fact, very cleansing to be able to talk about oneself using straightforward language. We do not have to be proud of our sinfulness, but it is comforting to know that when we acknowledge our sinfulness in a direct and obvious manner, we are standing shoulder to shoulder with all the saints of the Church, not with the sinners; it is the saints who are honestly aware of their own unworthiness before the throne of God, not the others.

In the process of growing up, it is very difficult to avoid conflicts with one's parents, brothers and sisters, and other significant figures. We perceive and adopt attitudes from family members, from teachers and others which generally affect the way we think about almost everything, and we do so without examining those attitudes very carefully. Sometimes in the course of a Fourth Step it is necessary to examine our attitudes about all sorts of things, and to decide whether those attitudes have led us toward God or away from Him. Some of our attitudes surface as beliefs, but others are no more than prejudices. Step Four makes it quite obvious that we are responsible for them all, the moment we choose to act on them. We cannot claim some sort of immunity from the effects of our attitudes, simply because we cannot remember where they came from.

A very strange phenomenon that still baffles me stems from the fact that people sometimes find themselves holding certain attitudes, and even prejudices, that they have adopted from another person, even when that other person has contributed more harm than good to the individual's life. I am thinking in particular of a woman who had an alcoholic mother whom she learned to hate. However, the daughter adopted a great number of her mother's attitudes. In trying to sort out that situation, she had to look very closely at the demands of Step Four, and pry away her mother's influence from her own sense of being a person.

Attitudes are very difficult to deal with. One of the great educators in the field of alcoholism, Fr. Joseph Martin, once made a remark that our attitudes are stronger than the rest of us put together—so strong, in fact, that they can survive the death of the body. It is imperative in recovery that all our attitudes are brought under examination.

It is no mistake that the letters AA can also stand for "Altered Attitudes."

In preparing for Step Four, it is quite important for us to be aware that some of the greatest sinners in the history of the Church went on to become great saints. When David the King gave us the life-changing words of that best-loved psalm (Psalm 51), "Have mercy on me, O God," it was because he had committed a sin of great and terrible proportions: he had sent a man to certain death, in order to continue an improper relationship with the man's wife. Nevertheless, through the grace of God his repentance was so great, so thorough, that King David went on to become one of the greatest heroes of the Old Testament.

Much nearer to us in time, St. Peter is not known as "St. Peter the Denier," even though his fainthearedness, when he denied that he knew Jesus, was a very serious matter. His act of weakness was not the end of the story, however, and eventually St. Peter went on to become the greatest leader of the early Church. St. Paul, his companion as leader of the Apostles, committed terrible violence against the Church before he changed his life, yet went on to become the most influential Apostle of the developing Church.

The level of sanctity reached by St. Mary of Egypt is difficult to match at any time in the history of the Church; even though her sinfulness was very great, her ascetic life of repentance was of a degree which few can even imagine, let alone emulate. She is, perhaps, particularly worthy of attention, since her sanctity is almost entirely due to her spirit of repentance. She will be considered at greater length in Step Ten.

There are several times in the life of an Orthodox Christian when it might be a good idea to make a general confession—that is, a confession which refers to events from one's entire life, including topics that have been mentioned in previous confessions. This is not actually necessary in terms of our relationship with God, because God's forgiveness is total and absolute. Since we are often less willing to accept God's forgiveness than God is to forgive us, however, such general confessions are often useful—for us, not for God.

When an adult comes for Holy Baptism in the Orthodox Church, or is received by the Holy Sacrament of Chrismation, it is normal for that person to make a general confession. Other times when it might be suitable would be before monastic profession, marriage, or ordination, and at times of serious sickness. Whenever this takes place, we need to be as thorough as we need to be, but we are generally cautioned not to be too hard on ourselves, and not to exaggerate the extent of our wrongdoing. Clarity, not condemnation, is required.

The purpose of a general confession and of Step Five is very similar. In both cases they allow the person to free himself from feelings of guilt which are the result of accumulated wrongdoing; they also allow the sponsor, or the priest, to gain an insight into the life of the person concerned.

The prodigal son seems ever present and is able to help us come to terms with Step Five. At the moment when he meets his father, he says: "Father, I have sinned against heaven and before you, and I am no longer worthy to be called your son" (Luke 15:18–19). This is the essence of Step Five.

✠ ✠ ✠ ✠ ✠ ✠ ✠ ✠

THE CRY OF THE PSALMIST gives us encouragement:

I said, "Lord, be merciful to me;
Heal my soul, for I have sinned against You" (Psalm 41:4).

And one of the daily prayers of the Church:

O God, remit, pardon, and forgive our sins, both voluntary and involuntary, in word or deed, in knowledge or in ignorance, whether by day or by night, whether in mind or thought: forgive us all of these, for You are good and You love mankind.

Chapter 11

Ready To Change

Step 6: Were entirely ready to have God remove all these defects of character.

Step 7: Humbly asked Him to remove our shortcomings.

Likewise you also, reckon yourselves to be dead indeed to sin, but alive to God in Christ Jesus our Lord. (Romans 6:11)

Put off, concerning your former conduct, the old man which grows corrupt according to the deceitful lusts, and be renewed in the spirit of your mind. (Ephesians 4:22, 23)

Rest in the Lord, and wait patiently for Him. (Psalm 37:7)

These two Steps are entirely unlike the rest of the Steps, for several reasons. They lie, more or less, at the halfway point, and they call not for a decision, not for an action, but for a state of mind.

The Sixth Step does not say, "We made ourselves entirely ready," but that "We *were* ready."

Like the spiritual life the Steps encourage, this particular Step is completely beyond our control. That is what makes it so crucial, and in a way so mystical. It cannot happen if we try to make it happen. It can only happen when we allow it to happen. This Step is a distillation of all the Steps put together. It can only take place after a nascent spirituality has been fostered in the preceding Steps.

Significance for an Addicted Person

Although it may seem obvious to the rest of the world, the alcoholic does not realize that the power outside himself is actually capable of doing anything unless he is made to do so. Once the idea has been sown that there is a power greater than himself, the concept needs to develop into something that is actually meaningful in the life of the recovering person. God is slowly allowed into the life of that person, but there is naturally a tacit assumption that this relationship is going to be like every other relationship in the alcoholic's life—he (the alcoholic) is going to have to manipulate and control the other person, if he is to get any benefit out of the encounter. It is with this Step that the notion finally arrives that God is a completely independent, powerful force, and that the person in recovery has nothing to do but to stand ready, waiting for God to act. It also marks the point where the alcoholic is beginning to come to an understanding that God can, if He chooses, do anything.

For the Orthodox Christian

I waited patiently for the Lord;
And He inclined to me,
And heard my cry. (Psalm 40:1)

Waiting for God to act is, in some ways, the natural state of the saint, and the learned behavior of the person who is experiencing spiritual growth. Waiting is also the natural state of the Church. "My eyes fail while I wait for my God" (Psalm 69:3). We have been in the last days ever since the Holy Spirit descended at Pentecost, and this is expressed in the Church's waiting. The life of the Church is an eternal vigil, watching and waiting for the Bridegroom to return.

Even so, waiting is not a passive activity—simply a void which God, in His own time, will fill. Waiting is filled with activity, not something barren and sterile. Waiting is already full of the love of God. There is a constant and unending stream of information coming from God to the Church and to the individual during this period.

There is a good deal of information given and received about personal matters—matters of the head and matters of the heart—all the things that make up our life: feelings, thoughts, facts, and figures. Some of this information requires a response on our part; much of it does not.

While we are waiting, God sustains and cares for us. He provides us with an environment for our physical life to develop, and endows us with what is needed for our spiritual lives to develop also. The correct atmospheric pressure is as much a result of God's love for us as is the opportunity to learn patience from some particular trial in our lives. God is interested even in the tiny details; He certainly cannot be unconcerned with the things that challenge us.

One of the paradoxes of human existence is that there is nowhere God is not. Even though we naturally assume that He is more concerned with certain parts of our lives than with others, God is not nearly as restrictive as we are. One of the closest analogies I have come across is that God is fascinated with us—who we are and what we do. No detail of our lives is too small for His infinite interest.

We cannot brush against God without being changed. In the case of the woman who was healed when she touched Jesus surreptitiously in the crowd, the encounter with God changed her life. So it is with us. Every meeting with God, no matter how casual or seemingly insignificant, involves both judgment and transformation.

✤ ✤ ✤ ✤ ✤ ✤ ✤ ✤

When the public part of the Divine Liturgy is about to start, after the priest has said the preparatory prayers, dressed himself in the sacred vestments, cut and prepared the bread, poured and mixed the wine, he prays the prayer of oblation. At this point the deacon, if there is one, says: "*Kairos tou poiesai to Kyrio*": "It is time for the Lord to act."

Like the words of the Sixth Step, this is both a statement and a prayer; it is a statement of fact and an act of faith. God acts; God takes part. Not because He can be controlled by the bidding of a mere human, but out of His inexhaustible love for humankind, He participates in the life of each person as that person reaches out towards his or her Creator.

✤ ✤ ✤ ✤ ✤ ✤ ✤ ✤

ONE OF THE MORE IMPORTANT ASPECTS of prayer is simply to get out of God's way. This is what this Step does. The degree to which a person is able to "let go, and let God" is the degree to which this Step is successful or not. It cannot be measured in any way; there is nothing to measure. The action is entirely taken by God, and the work of the person doing the Step is to allow it to happen.

It is at this point that the individual comes to an awareness that although he is doing the Steps, the work of the Steps is actually the work of God. This sense of being in direct cooperation with God is very profound, and helps the individual to come to the conclusion that God takes an interest in the most insignificant details of that person's life. However, God's action can be, and often is, limited by the individual concerned, to whom God has given the power of veto in the form of freedom.

Most people grow up thinking that there may be a God, but that His influence is either very, very small, or is held in reserve until something really important comes along. People may agonize over big decisions, and ask God to guide them in the choice of a spouse, a new job, or a new home. Strangely, too, we seem to assume that there are certain areas where the intervention of God would not be beneficial. We often try to interest God in a list of sick people and the world's political problems, but just as carefully we try to keep Him away from areas concerning sex or bank balances.

Most prayers that start, "Dear God, please . . ." are not answered —at least, not in the most direct way. If they were, there would only be one religion, and everyone would belong to it. That would be a chaotic world in which the human ego, with its bottomless desires, would be king.

We tend to reserve prayer for big decisions, and then take the consequences, as if the outcome of the prayer does not matter at all.

The idea that prayer is the nature of the relationship that governs everything in a person's life, right down to the smallest detail, is a new idea, and this is what needs to be assimilated at this Step. God is involved with the tiniest detail; each nuance, each thought, each feeling is available for the relationship with God to be made manifest.

Step 7. Humbly asked Him to remove our shortcomings.

Humble yourselves under the mighty hand of God, that He may exalt you in due time, casting all your care upon Him, for He cares for you. (1 Peter 5:6–7)

Behold, I stand at the door and knock. If anyone hears My voice and opens the door, I will come in to him and dine with him, and he with Me. (Revelation 3:20)

Ask, and it will be given to you; seek, and you will find; knock, and it will be opened to you. (Matthew 7:7)

Significance for an Addicted Person

In the Big Book, this Step is introduced with the prayer:

My Creator, I am now willing that you should have all of me, good and bad. I pray that you now remove from me every single defect of character which stands in the way of my usefulness to you and my fellows. Grant me strength, as I go out from here, to do your bidding. Amen. (*Alcoholics Anonymous,* p. 76)

The alcoholic is so used to living with his own inadequacies that it is likely he is convinced that he is going to be stuck with whatever character attributes he has, and that he just needs to learn to live with that fact. This Step comes to terms with the central idea that although the alcoholic may have been released from the compulsion to drink, and his life may have started to improve, nevertheless he is still under the apprehension that he cannot change, and that apart from stopping drinking, nothing much will alter. In the thinking of AA, however, this is not possible, because it does not supply the whole picture. Drinking is merely a symptom of a disorder within the personality, not the disease itself. The disease must be confronted, it must be treated and medicated, or the symptom will return once again.

The confrontation with the disease takes place in Step Seven.

Drinking alcoholics live with a curious, yet deadly, mixture of pride and self-hatred. They can trust only themselves, and they cannot trust themselves. They defend themselves with every ounce of energy they can muster, but they also know that they are not worth it, that they are beneath contempt. Naturally, the drinker tends to associate this meeting of feelings with his drinking, and almost every alcoholic has a sense at some point that if only he could stop drinking, everything else would be all right. However, once the alcoholic stops drinking, and he starts to do the Steps, it becomes more and more obvious that he has to work very hard to keep and develop his sobriety. Getting drunk is a passive activity: you simply pour enough alcohol down your throat, and your body, mind, and spirit will do the rest. Getting sober requires healing—in body, mind, and spirit—and the healing comes with a price, and the price for that healing is willingness.

At the point where the alcoholic thinks that there is nothing much that can be done about his condition, a new idea is introduced. It is introduced so slowly, so subtly, that he might not even notice it. Often on reading the Twelve Steps, Steps Six and Seven slip by with very little notice. In fact, they are the heart of the program, a mystical high point. By this time, the relationship with the Higher Power is in place, and starting to grow. Now it is put to the test. God is asked to change the character of the person doing the Steps.

Of course, the Step says nothing about how God will do this, or in what way He will accomplish it. That is entirely within God's prerogative, and the Steps are very careful not to suggest that it is possible—at any point—to predict the mind of God.

It is fairly certain that if someone were to say to the drinker: "Stop drinking!" the command would be ignored, or incorporated into whatever systems of defense the alcoholic has developed to keep himself and his drinking safe. If that same person should say to the alcoholic, "Stop drinking, then allow yourself to be changed beyond recognition," the command would not only be ignored, but would probably be subject to derision. However, that is precisely what this

Step does. This is the change that needs to take place so that whatever sobriety already exists might take root and grow.

It is a characteristic of the Steps that the most demanding and the most difficult tasks are often slipped into the text with no fanfare. Here is the big one, however. This is where the recovery happens. Here God is asked to change the personality of the alcoholic. And this is where God does just that.

This process does not render the individual perfect, however. There is still much to be done. In the general philosophical outlook of the Steps, it is progress, not perfection, that is sought. Perfection is limited to God alone, and yet the action of God within the personality draws the individual towards goodness.

For the Orthodox Christian
Take from me the spirit of sloth, of meddling, of lust for power and idle chatter. (Prayer of Saint Ephraim)

This is the Step at which to look carefully at some other aspects of the way we use the Sacrament of Confession.

During my life as an Orthodox Christian, I have come across a wide variety of views concerning the Sacrament of Confession. In some traditions, confession is considered to be the essential preparation for Holy Communion, and frequent, sometimes even weekly, confession is the norm. Admittedly, this tends to be in churches that have been most influenced by Russian tradition. I attended the Divine Liturgy in Finland many years ago, before I was ordained, and I approached the Chalice at the time for Holy Communion. Since the priest did not recognize me, I was led to the side by a young altar server. Another priest then came and heard my confession—while the rest of the congregation waited. The problem was that the priest and I had no common language: he spoke Finnish and Swedish, and I did not. Eventually, I was asked to kneel, and I felt the priest's stole on my head, and a prayer was read. Only then was I free to approach the Chalice and receive Holy Communion.

I had a completely different reaction from another priest at about the same time. I went to a church on the South Coast of England where almost all the parishioners were from Cyprus. Since I did not know the priest, I made a point of getting to the service early, and asked to see him. He emerged from the altar, but made it quite plain that he was rather busy, and had better things to do. Nevertheless, I asked him if I might receive Communion at the Liturgy. He looked puzzled. "Can't you just come up with all the rest?" he said.

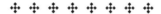

GENERALLY, WHERE THERE IS A PRACTICE of going to confession frequently, the sacrament is seen as a pastoral opportunity for the priest and the penitent to look into different aspects of the penitent's life. The person making the confession talks in fairly general terms about his faults, freely volunteering the information, listing small matters together with large ones. It is possible that the priest might question the person about certain things, particularly to clarify what is being said. People frequently use euphemisms in confession, or a sort of churchlike language, sometimes to the point where it is difficult to be clear about what the person is actually saying. At the end the priest generally talks in a kindly fashion, encouraging where it is needed, stressing that all men are sinners and that it is necessary to allow God's love to shine through in spite of our weaknesses. After that the priest prays the prayers of absolution. The wording of the prayer in the Russian tradition is heavily influenced by Roman Catholic thinking, and contains a declaration of forgiveness in the direct form, "I forgive you."

In other churches, generally those of the Greek tradition, confession is often considered in an entirely different light. To begin with, confession is not necessarily considered to be a preparation for the reception of Holy Communion. Holy Communion and confession are quite separate sacraments. The essential preparation for receiving Holy Communion in this tradition tends to be fasting. Moreover, confession is thought of as being something reserved for serious sins, and is a matter of great consequence. One goes to confession quite expecting to be given a stern series of warnings, and even to be questioned in detail about one's sins. There are prayers of absolution, and they are read, although often with less obvious ceremony than in the Russian tradition, and the wording of the prayers lacks the directness of the prayer of absolution in the Russian tradition.

Incidentally, when there are different traditions within the Orthodox Church, as there certainly are in the case of confession, people coming to the Church from other faiths should take care to conform with the general norms practiced within the diocese they have chosen. There is no point in accusing the Russians of not being Greeks, or vice versa. The Church is large enough to bear a number of different traditions in many areas of its life, and it is for the individual to accept, not to judge.

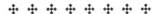

YEARS AGO, I HAPPENED TO BE on Mount Athos and in a situation where, because of a particular set of circumstances, I wanted to go to confession. Being used to the traditions of the little Orthodox church in Oxford, I expected to be met with kindness and encouragement. Instead, the priest (he was actually an abbot) brushed off my attempt to talk of the things I wanted to talk about and started cross-examining me about my life, about sexual matters in general, and about explicit sexual matters in particular, some of which I found quite offensive. For him it was like a yes/no quiz, followed by a stern lecture. He proceeded to give me a long talk on the relative values of the Greek and British ways of life, in which the country of my birth did not fare well. I was bitterly disappointed, and left feeling violated. Naturally, this priest was simply following the tradition to which he was accustomed—after all, in his thinking, why would I go to confession, if that is not what I expected—yet I left hurt, saddened, and greatly disillusioned.

Nevertheless, the Greek practice, characterized here, actually seems to be much more in tune with the practice of the early Church. In the first centuries of the Christian era, sins committed after baptism, necessarily those of a serious nature, were confessed in public, and the punishment (penance) was a public matter also, visible and obvious to all, even to the point of being incorporated into the architecture of a typical Byzantine church.

On entering a traditional Orthodox church building, the worshippers pass through an area called the narthex (and sometimes a preliminary "outer narthex" as well). Nowadays, the main function of this area is to house the candlestands and the icons that are venerated by the people before they enter the church proper. In monasteries and very traditional communities, some of the services, particularly the Lity at Vespers (and sometimes in Orthros, too), as well as some parts of the Sacraments of Marriage and Baptism, take place in this area also. However, it is well to remember that this part of the church was used for hundreds of years as the place for those who were under penance (and there were several different levels or grades of penance practiced), who were not allowed to enter the sanctuary proper with the rest of the congregation, and not even allowed to see the altar area. The numbers of those under penance standing in the narthex were augmented by the presence of the catechumens and others who were not yet members of the Church. In some ancient texts it seems quite apparent that, at least in the largest churches, the narthex was a large area, packed with people; of necessity those in the narthex would be seen by all those who had the right to enter into the main body of the church as they passed through. One can quite well imagine that emotions could easily be highly charged in that situation.

Public penance is largely a thing of the past in the Orthodox Church, except in the cases of excommunication of lay people and the defrocking of clergy. Even though some rules and regulations which are often published with collections of the Canons of the Church mention many sins for which fixed penances have been imposed at one time or another during the history of the Church, this is rarely practiced in the modern world.

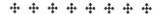

Notice that the wording in Step Seven is not explicitly and solely to do with forgiveness, although that is obviously a part of it. Even for people who have a relatively good state of mental health, it seems much easier for God to forgive than for us to receive His forgiveness. That is perhaps why Jesus first showed the crowd how He was able to make a paralyzed man walk (something they could see), in order to show them that He was able to forgive sins (the effects of which they could not see). We often need to reflect on that.

God's forgiveness needs to be accepted before it is of any value to us. It is useful to consider that forgiveness is a fact, a declaration, a piece of information, not a feeling. If we wait to feel that we have been forgiven, it often means that we have lost the sense that what we did actually needed to be forgiven in the first place. When we forgive each other, as we are asked to do frequently in our Church life, it is important to remember there too that forgiveness is not a feeling, but a decision. Our feelings may—or may not—match our decision to forgive. In fact, forgiveness is likely to be more significant when it runs counter to our feelings. If we say "I forgive you" and feel nothing, it likely means that what we are actually saying is that we have forgotten some particular wrong, not that we are forgiving it. When our feelings are outraged, our decision to forgive is usually much more significant. Our feelings may (or may not) catch up with our decision—but they do not affect the forgiveness, or cause it in any way.

STEP SEVEN TALKS OF THE REMOVAL OF OUR SHORTCOMINGS, not the forgiveness of sins. This throws a particularly strong light on the difference between religion and spirituality as defined by the Twelve Steps. "Removal of shortcomings" can be accepted as a concept by men of all religions or none, whereas forgiveness of sins presupposes a developed awareness of both sin and forgiveness.

Jesus' frequent commandment in the Gospel, "Go and sin no more," has exactly the sense of removing someone's defects of character. In words and in deeds, it is expected that the person is going to change. True, he might turn up with the same faults a few days later, but for that moment, there is a sense in which the encounter with God, whether in the Step or in Confession, results in his being changed or transformed.

It is in Step Seven that all the mysteries revealed in Step Four regarding resentments, people-pleasing, caretaking, fear of authority, and all the others, are solved. These are the very items we ask God to remove from us, on a daily basis, for the rest of our lives.

"I said: Lord, have mercy on me; heal my soul, for I have sinned against You" (the Great Doxology).

The Prayer of Saint Ephraim is one of the most loved of the huge numbers of prayers available to the Orthodox Christian. It is recognized at once as the prayer which is often accompanied by prostrations. The act of prostration is good for the soul, and good for the body. However, the action should never detract from the very important words of the prayer itself, which are in every way suitable to be recited as a prayer for the Seventh Step:

Lord and Master of my life,
Take from me the spirit of sloth, of meddling, of lust for
     power and idle chatter.
Give to me rather the spirit of integrity, humility, patience,
     and love.
Yes, King and Master—grant me to see my own sins and
     not to judge my brother, for You are blessed to the ages
     of ages, Amen.

Chapter 12

Making Amends

Step 8: Made a list of all persons we had harmed, and became willing to make amends to them all.

Step 9: Made direct amends to such people wherever possible, except when to do so would injure them or others.

Blessed are the peacemakers, / For they shall be called sons of God. (Matthew 5:9)

Therefore if you bring your gift to the altar, and there remember that your brother has something against you, leave your gift there before the altar, and go your way. First be reconciled to your brother, and then come and offer your gift. (Matthew 5:23, 24)

Love your enemies, bless those who curse you, do good to those who hate you, and pray for those who spitefully use you and persecute you. (Matthew 5:44)

Significance for an Addicted Person

Honesty is an important lesson for the recovering alcoholic, principally because the drinking alcoholic's native environment is lies and deceit. That is where he feels most happy and most safe. Remember that an alcoholic will often tell a lie rather than the truth, because he can "control" the lie, whereas the truth is beyond his control. A lie can be anything he wants it to be, whereas the truth comes ready-made.

According to popular wisdom, often heard in AA meetings, there are three criteria for judging whether something needs to be said or not, and these criteria are particularly useful in determining whether certain things have to be offered by way of amends in Step Eight. For any statement to be authentic or legitimate, the statement has to be *true*, it has to be *necessary*, and it has to be *kind*. Actually, this is a good set of criteria by which to judge any statement, made by anyone, at any time. Conversely, if by applying these criteria we find we have nothing left to say, then we need to review our entire mode of speaking.

Once they get hold of a concept, alcoholics are in danger of viewing it in a very black-and-white manner. In particular, the alcoholic has to learn that although something may be true, it is not necessarily the right or ethical thing to tell that truth. This is very difficult for him. In the wording of the Steps, particularly here with Step Nine, it is stated that it is important to tell the truth (here about harms, real or imagined, inflicted on others), unless that truth actually causes more harm, in which case we should refrain from doing anything. This restricts us from using the Steps to justify behavior that, while posing as a desire to make amends (or ask forgiveness), would, in fact, inflict greater pain than that which it sought to relieve, and have the nature of punishment instead of seeking to make amends.

Because of the way the human mind works, it is quite possible that under the guise of making amends to someone, we could actually cause them harm. Such might happen, for example, if a person had committed adultery years before, but the affair had ended with no further complications. However, when he came to get sober, then got ready to do Step Eight, this same person felt it was necessary to tell the husband of his former lover about the affair, in order to make amends. This would not be making amends; it might be true, but it would actually be causing pain, and is thus not allowed.

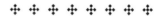

HONESTY IS NOT THE BEST POLICY. Honesty is the *only* policy. Honesty for its own sake is required at every level of the recovering person's life, mainly to combat the fact that dishonesty is so easy. Being honest all the time requires great effort, particularly if it was regarded as unseemly, dangerous, or simply inconvenient in one's family of origin. In alcoholic families, for example, where the father is a drinker, the fact that he drinks, and the fact that he causes problems when he does so, may never be a subject for discussion or even comment. In this way, children learn that there are certain topics which may not be discussed, and they simply erase them from the list of things they talk about.

Shame might also cause people to bend their world into a vision which is not quite true. I well remember a family in one of my former parishes in which the mother was often admitted to inpatient care for treatment for a nervous disorder. I liked them all very much, but there was an unspoken family rule that mental illness was simply not acknowledged. Her illness was never mentioned, never discussed, and any enquiry on my part was met with blank looks and a change of subject.

There may be a great variety of topics which a particular family (most likely influenced by a powerful figure within that family) simply ignores as if they are not there. Children who learn to step over the body of a drunk parent without comment eventually learn to feel nothing, and later still, to see nothing. They have already learned to say nothing. This is a very dangerous situation. It leads to whole families living in denial.

There are examples in history where entire nations have lived in denial. Nazi Germany is a case in point. Although it was quite obvious from many points of view that Hitler and his followers were very evil, there was almost no organized voice of opposition to Nazi rule, because opposition was made too dangerous. Almost no one raised a voice to state the obvious, and so what was "obvious" was bent—a distorted vision, to which everyone paid at least lip service.

Honesty smashes through denial. This is well illustrated by the little boy in the story of the emperor who was persuaded that his clothes were so fine they could only be seen by people who were really intelligent. Although the emperor knew he could not see them himself, he assumed that all those around him could see them, and to make any comment would be to betray his own lack of intelligence. Naturally all the others assumed the emperor *could* see the clothes, and that it was only their own lack of intelligence which stopped them from seeing them too. This is a perfect icon of denial. Of course, no one could actually see the clothes, because there weren't any. It took the guileless confidence of a little boy to call out that the emperor was, in fact, naked.

Even in countries that are run along very democratic lines, bosses of companies, teachers, military officers, and sometimes even political and religious leaders who are wholly unfit to do the work they do are surrounded by people like those in the story, who have long ago decided that it is better to say nothing, rather than risk being treated as a troublemaker.

For the individual doing the Steps, the cost of honesty might be very considerable, involving making great changes just to live in an environment where honesty can rule.

MAKING AMENDS IS NOT THE SAME as saving the world or transforming the life of the person to whom the amends are being made. Sometimes that person will hardly notice, and sometimes (for example, when the person has already died or moved away) it will not be possible to make amends other than symbolically. The important principle here is that we do not actually make amends to others *for their sake*, but *for our own*. The quality of those amends is important, the response essentially irrelevant.

A further area some people find difficult is that they assume that if they are recovering from alcoholism, the amends are to be made to those whom they hurt during their alcoholism. This is only partly true. Step Eight and Step Nine are more effective if they include all the harm the person has ever inflicted on another.

For the Orthodox Christian
When Zacchaeus stood and said to the Lord, "Look, Lord, I give half of my goods to the poor; and if I have taken anything from anyone by false accusation, I restore fourfold," he was doing Step Nine.

What Zacchaeus did was to go beyond the requirements of the Law of Moses, in a spirit of love and gratitude. Christians should follow his example. Furthermore, in making amends we should not be concerned with any wrongs people have done to us—even if they are the same people to whom we are making amends.

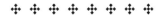

OF THE MANY WONDERFUL MEMORIES I have of my early contacts with the Orthodox Church, one of the strongest was a Vespers service I attended at the little Orthodox church in Oxford. I was a student at the university at the time, and had come across the Orthodox church when I, together with some of the other students from my college, decided to visit some of the more important churches in Oxford on Sunday mornings, after attending the more-or-less compulsory service at our own college chapel.

The first week we visited an Anglican church at which a delightful, quietly eccentric priest led a service in which both he and the congregation acted as if the Reformation had never quite reached England. The church had an almost Italian spirituality mixed, oddly, with a large dose of English reserve.

The second week we visited the Orthodox church. At that time, this community (or rather communities—one Greek Orthodox, the other Russian Orthodox) was still worshipping in the tiny room which, in rather grander days, had been the library of the famous Dr. Spooner.[13] As soon as I entered the small, incense-filled space, I immediately felt at home. I left my friends to continue visiting other churches on subsequent Sundays, but I had found what I was looking for, even though I never had a clear idea that I was actually looking. Three years later, I was received into the Orthodox Church.

I started to attend this little church frequently, and quite soon I

---

13 Dr. W. A. Spooner (1844–1930) was Warden of New College, Oxford. He is famous for making misstatements involving transposition of initial sounds, such as "the queer old dean" for "the dear old queen"—hence "Spoonerisms."

joined the choir, which meant I had to come to terms with a great deal of Slavonic, as well as a little Greek. I became actively acquainted with the way Orthodox services are put together, and I began to appreciate the huge range of the liturgical life of the Orthodox Church.

In due course I attended the Vespers service that marks the beginning of Great Lent. In Oxford, as happens in most Russian churches and Greek monasteries, there was a service called "Vespers of Forgiveness." At the end of the service, the parish priest came out from behind the icon screen and quietly and seriously asked the congregation to forgive him for any of his actions that might have caused them hurt. There followed a little ceremony in which each member of the congregation approached and prostrated himself in front of the priest, asking for forgiveness. The priest did the same thing, before arising and sealing the process by blessing the person. The person then stood to the right of the priest, and each subsequent member of the congregation then came forward and prostrated in front of the priest, then in front of the person standing on his right; each was met with a mutual prostration, and a mutual request for forgiveness. The action was completed with a threefold kiss, and so each member of the congregation approached every other member of the congregation, and much forgiveness was given and received.

For me, one of the most moving elements of this service was that it was attended by some very important and senior members of the university. I found myself kneeling in front of them and asking their forgiveness, but they were actually doing the same thing to me. Under most circumstances, and certainly in other universities around the world, these were people with whom I would hardly have had a chance to talk. In this context, however, it gave great depth to my growing experience of Orthodoxy.

Naturally such a ceremony can become an empty symbol. I clearly remember years later meeting two monks living in the same monastery who disliked each other so severely that they had a mutual agreement to miss each other out in such ceremonies. However, what I found in Oxford was both a remarkable example of humility and an important example of the practicality of spiritual life.

The Ninth Step is a nonreligious version of the Vespers of Forgiveness.

At a number of points in the Divine Liturgy, the priest turns to the people and bows. In the preparatory prayers, before the Great Entrance, and again before receiving Holy Communion, he asks the people for their forgiveness, and promises to forgive them also.

Asking for forgiveness is a very normal and important part of the Christian life, not as a punishment, but enjoyed in freedom by the children of God. This is particularly important before we approach the Holy Chalice to receive Holy Communion. Our Lord explicitly tells us that seeking and giving forgiveness is a prerequisite to receiving the Body and Blood of Christ at the altar. We cannot be fully present in the presence of the Lord if we are out of harmony with our brothers and sisters.

Making amends to people who have died is done by praying for them. This is true, too, of anyone whom we cannot actually contact in person. Anyone who can be contacted in person should be approached and told why it is necessary to speak to them. Naturally, we are not responsible for their reaction. They may be friendly, they may be scornful. However, if we have done our part properly, we have taken Step Nine.

Chapter 13

Keeping Clean

Step 10: Continued to take personal inventory and when we were wrong promptly admitted it.

Watch and pray, lest you enter into temptation. The spirit indeed is willing, but the flesh is weak. (Mark 14:38)

Forgive us our sins, / For we also forgive everyone who is indebted to us. (Luke 11:4)

As far as the east is from the west, / So far has He removed our transgressions from us. (Psalm 103:12)

Significance for an Addicted Person

Once the bulk of the work of the Steps has been done, it has the effect of wiping the slate clean. The alcoholic has learned to face God, to face himself and then the rest of the world. He has no more skeletons in the closets of his past, and although there may be remnants of feeling—usually shame or regret—nevertheless, he is walking a new life. The past is over, and so long as he does not drink again, he need never go back to it.

Having cleaned the house of his soul, he needs to devise a way of keeping it clean. Step Ten is designed to do just that. Personal inventory, once applied to the whole of his life (in Step Four), is now applied with the same sort of rigor, but one day at a time.

Naturally, some of the things that seemed to dominate Step Four will, by this stage, no longer be a problem. Almost certainly, the alcoholic will have stopped drinking by this point, and the obvious behaviors that go along with drinking will have disappeared. Remember, though, that for the alcoholic, drinking is merely the tip of the iceberg—a very obvious tip, but a tip nevertheless. The mass of turmoil that feeds his active alcoholism is very susceptible to the way the recovering alcoholic looks at himself or feels about himself. This is where he needs to recognize what he is doing wrong, and learn how to deal with it to the point that doing so becomes an instinctive reaction.

In the wording of the Step, the recovering person is told to recognize, then to admit to his wrongs. It would not be out of place to acknowledge the things he is doing right as well—a moral inventory has a plus side as well as a negative one. However, it is his mistakes and wrongs that are going to come back to haunt him, and they are the ones that *must* be included.

Taking a daily inventory, preferably towards the end of the day, is a good way of taking one's spiritual temperature. It allows one to look into a number of factors, including one's mood, one's prayer-life, and one's relationships with others. It is a time to review areas where we have been trying particularly hard: use of money or time, use of language, and taking part in unnecessary talking and similar activities. As such, the exercise is good for anyone. For the alcoholic, wanting to stay sober, it is a necessity.

For the Orthodox Christian

Sometimes we need to see things in an extreme form before we take much notice. When things are done in moderation, they tend to slip us by.

This is perhaps why the Church sets aside one Sunday a year, during Great Lent, to look at the example given to us by St. Mary of Egypt. By any criterion, St. Mary led an extreme sort of life, first in her profligacy, then in her repentance.

St. Mary spent many years in her youth leading a dissolute life. Her sins were mainly sexual in nature, and there is also a naturalness about her with which most people can find some degree of identification, even if only in imagination. When she happened to go to Jerusalem, she underwent a profound experience upon trying to enter the Church of the Holy Sepulcher. As a result of this experience, she spent the rest of her life in the Judean desert in circumstances of extreme asceticism.

The motivation for her new life was to seek forgiveness for the sins she had committed, and that she did with great fervor. However, in the process, her hard work and devotion brought her a life that was supernatural, filled with vision and an awareness of the presence of God. Her unquenchable physical desire was transformed into an insatiable thirst for God. Her appetites for food and drink were transformed into a longing for Holy Communion. Attacked by evil and dangerous temptations, she struggled and struggled until she prevailed; in the end she was bothered by neither heat nor cold, and was fed directly by the Word of God.

St. Mary of Egypt is a hero of the whole Church, but particularly for monastics, who try to emulate at least a part of her effort and enthusiasm for God. She demonstrates a way of life nearer to that of an angel than that of a human being, and this is one of the visions that gives life to the monastic ideal.

Lay people are not monastics, but their state of life is as blessed and fruitful as that of any monastic, although perhaps in less obvious ways. Nevertheless, laymen and laywomen are encouraged to become familiar with the life of the monastery, to visit, to listen, to take part in the monastic life, at least for short periods of time.

Like the Steps, the monastic path involves a radical reevaluation of the values of human society. Right from the start, the ego is laid aside, and through prayer and fasting, through discipline and effort, the monastic person makes his way to God. Awareness of sin in our daily lives is an important element of the process of *metanoia*, or repentance, and as each sin is admitted, so the path becomes more and more engaging.

In Orthodox terminology, the call to the priesthood is less a matter of "vocation"—of an inner call to that high office—than it is to do with the needs of the Church in any given time. Essentially a person is ordained to the priesthood because the Church needs that person to be a priest, not because that person feels called to the priesthood. A person cannot "give himself" to the priesthood, according to this way of thinking. Rather, the priesthood is something God bestows on him.

On the other hand, everyone is theoretically capable of entering the monastic life, and anyone may, unless to do so would inflict hardship on anyone who happens to be in that person's care. In monasticism there is an offering of self—an offering of one's freedom, an offering of one's life and will—to God.

Most members of the Church are not going to become monks and nuns in the near future at least, and the offering of oneself to the monastic life is always going to be something unusual, something out of the ordinary. However, everyone can participate, at least in part, in the spirit of monasticism by participating in Step Ten. Compared with monastic life, it may seem a small thing. However, by so doing we are linking ourselves to the immense amount of monastic wisdom and spiritual strength which the monasteries bring to the life of the Church.

At the service of monastic profession, the person to be made a monk stands in front of the monastic superior. Three times he is asked to pick up the scissors with which the superior is about to give him the tonsure—the cutting of the hair which marks the ending of this person's secular life and the beginning of his life as a monk. Sometimes, with some enthusiasm, the superior actually throws the scissors to the ground—an unfriendly gesture, to be sure, but one that makes it quite plain that the person who is about to enter the monastic family does so through his own desire, since it is his choice whether or not he picks up the scissors and returns them to the superior's hand.

In allowing his hair to be cut, the monastic beginner signifies that he is giving away his freedom—to the monastic superior, certainly, but in a much deeper and more important sense, to God Himself. Similarly, in baptism the individual accepts his new title "Slave of God" by allowing his hair to be cut.

In the Orthodox marriage service there is a ceremony that is the counterpart of this action. However, instead of the scissors, the husband and wife take each other and walk three times around the small wedding table, led by the priest, in whose hands are the Holy Gospels. Here the couple give their obedience to each other in the first place, and then place their entire relationship into the hands of God.

Orthodox thinking does not have a great deal to say about single people. A single person has no one in his life who obviously receives his obedience. In the monastic setting, the monk or nun belongs to the monastic family, and it is that family which cares for that person, even though the training and experience might be difficult. In the married state, the couple give each other their obedience, and in return care for each other, nurture each other, and promise to stay together even when things get difficult.

It is generally not good for us to be alone, but under certain circumstances, the Steps may be able to provide the single person with something like the structure and sense of responsibility that monks and nuns and married people naturally receive through their respective families. In belonging to a Twelve-Step group, there are many opportunities for spiritual intimacy that help to keep us on track, and give us the sense of direction others receive through the members of their respective families.

Step Ten is, in some ways, the essence of the Christian life, and the person who does Step Ten on a regular basis, even if not daily, is putting repentance into action, and treading the path of the angels.

Chapter 14

Getting To Know God

Step 11: Sought through prayer and meditation to improve our conscious contact with God as we understood Him, praying only for knowledge of His will for us and the power to carry that out.

> *Be anxious for nothing, but in everything by prayer and supplication, with thanksgiving, let your requests be made known to God.* (Philippians 4:6)

> *Now this is the confidence that we have in Him, that if we ask anything according to His will, He hears us.* (1 John 5:14)

> *Whatever things you ask in prayer, believing, you will receive.* (Matthew 21:22)

Significance for an Addicted Person

Once the miracle of sobriety is in place, the alcoholic needs to be aware that the ongoing sobriety he experiences is part of his relationship with God. God gives the grace to be sober, just as God gives life—one day at a time. What is required is to live in accordance with His will. We may never know, with a certainty, what that will is. It is the act of seeking of which we are capable—the act of praying, and it is that which we are asked to do.

Why the author of the Steps separated prayer from meditation is not entirely clear. Certainly, the Steps were written down before there was any mass-meditation movement such as happened during the Flower Power era. Bill W. was well read in many subjects, and it is possible that he had something very specific in mind. If he did, he says nothing about it, either in the Big Book or the Twelve and Twelve, where he seems to use the words interchangeably.

At the very least, we might make an inference that the two words "prayer" and "meditation" refer to the active and passive types of prayer, to speaking and listening. However, even that is not certain. What is important is that the recovering person sees prayer and meditation as the source of his meaning and of his strength. He does not acquire the mind of God, but reaches out towards Him. It is that act of reaching out which gives authenticity to his newfound life.

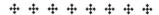

IT IS LIKELY, THOUGH NOT INEVITABLE, that if a person was religious before becoming alcoholic, he needs to review his religious thinking and behavior when he starts the recovery process. If we regard alcoholism as a spiritual disorder, it is almost certain that the person has, during the course of his addiction, used religious and spiritual themes in a broken or distorted way. This does not necessarily mean that there is anything wrong with his religion—it refers to his use of that religion. It almost certainly means that his view of God is dysfunctional. Drinking alcoholics know how to pray—at least they know how to try to do bargains with God. They possibly spend more time on their knees than the average monk, but the shrine they pray before is porcelain, and it does not usually have religious associations.

The alcoholic has to learn that the prayer and meditation which will be his lifeline in sobriety bear little, if any, resemblance to the activity he called prayer in the past. Apart from anything else, in the new circumstances, prayer ceases to be a "deal." It turns out that God does not seem to want to do deals very often. Furthermore, prayer has results. The alcoholic is used to shrieking prayers in heaven's direction, but without any sense at all that he is going to get a positive answer. He is used to God apparently ignoring him, cheating him, letting him down. Almost by definition, one might say that there is no relationship between God and the alcoholic—at least not of any personal kind. The alcoholic fluctuates between hating God and denying His existence, and God simply waits. Alcoholism, like everything that involves pain and suffering, everything that is cruel and depraved, everything that is sad and unjust, is part of the price God pays for giving us freedom.

Once the alcoholic has stopped trying to play God, he gently allows his mistaken and deadly worldview to be replaced by another. In this new worldview, there is a God, other than his own ego, who is the highest expression of existence. God's will has governed all creation for a very long time, and will continue to do so long after the alcoholic dies. His will is an expression of goodness and love, and is experienced by the entire universe in all its vastness, but also in the tiniest detail of the life of each person. A life worth living, a good life, a sober life, involves seeking the will of God and doing it. *Seeking*, not *knowing*, is important. Once the alcoholic thinks he *knows* the will of God, it is very easy for him to fall back into his old ways, and the result is that instead of having a broken life as a drunken man, he now has a broken life as a sober one.

When the alcoholic seeks the will of God, and tries with all his strength to carry it out (strength that, too, comes from God), he is doing what he is supposed to do. His life is full, made up of the little tasks that constitute the stuff of human existence, and he performs the demands on him, one task at a time. Sometimes the tasks will be small—seemingly insignificant—like washing his hands, or closing his eyes to go to sleep. Sometimes his tasks will be of a higher level—spending time in prayer or performing some service to others.

There is nothing passive about his relationship with God. He does not lie around waiting for God to speak to him from a tornado or a bolt of lightning. God meets him in the ordinary events of life, and the person learns to respond with humility and gratitude, under all circumstances. Never quite certain that he is doing what is required of him, yet knowing that God has a will for him, he is full of hope that he is doing just that. *Certainty* does not belong in the "safe zone" for the recovering alcoholic—it is too close to the sort of behavior which Bill W. calls "self-will run riot." Seeking is enough—it is enough.

For the Orthodox Christian

Step Eleven is an opportunity to evaluate what you are doing in your prayer life, and to ask some questions that rarely get asked. What do you pray for? What, or how, do you pray? Do you like to read prayers, or to be spontaneous? Do you actually pray at all? When you go to church, do you spend the whole time on matters that are of little (or, at least, secondary) importance? Do you pray morning and evening? Alone or with others?

What do you pray for? Sometimes, we have the tendency to give God a shopping list of what is wrong with His world, balanced with a perhaps not-too-discreet hint that He might like to run things better. Sometimes prayer becomes simply a list of grumbles at what we regard as the injustices of the world. If any of this is true, something needs to be done.

Our greatest lessons can be learned from the prayer-life of the Church, the Divine Liturgy and all the other services the Church possesses to sanctify people, time, and place. We do well to see exactly what we are doing in church, and then try to bring that experience into our own lives.

Before the beginning of the public parts of the Divine Liturgy, the priest says prayers, puts on the vestments, washes his hands, then goes to stand at the little altar of Offering, the Holy Prothesis. There he prepares the bread and the wine, cutting the bread in a particular way, as laid down in our traditions, and placing the pieces of bread on the Holy Diskos, the special dish we use for the bread.

When he has finished the formal and traditional parts of this preparation, the priest is then free to commemorate people by name. At each name or group of names, he cuts out a little piece of bread, and places it in the traditional place, beneath the rectangular piece of bread which will be changed into the Body of Christ. As he places each piece of bread he says: "Lord, remember *N*," placing the first (Christian) name of the person for whom he is praying in the place of the letter *N*. He may say very few names at this point, or he may say many thousands. Sometimes he will be asked by people in his pastoral care to remember particular people, and often a parish priest will have a list (often memorized, and often quite long) of all the members of the parish.

Members of the congregation are at liberty to bring lists of names for the priest to commemorate at this point, whether or not they have also baked a loaf of communion bread. The only problem is that they have to bring the lists early enough, since the priest should not stop the service to read long lists of names once the public part of the Liturgy ("Blessed is the Kingdom . . .") has started.

It is well known that certain bishops and priests have been known to read very many names at this point, and that is perfectly good, so long as they are not thereby inconveniencing the people with their personal devotions.

The priest prays simply: "Lord, remember *N*." He does not go on to ask anything in particular for that person. The prayer "Lord, remember" is sufficient, covers every eventuality, and is a beautiful expression of love. In terms of intercession, that is what prayer is: an expression of love. We are neither telling God something he does not already know, nor are we trying to twist His arm and make Him change His mind.

Whether the person being prayed for is alive or dead, the prayer, "Lord, remember" brings the person praying, the person prayed for, and God together.

In praying for groups of people, the litanies of the Divine Liturgy serve as a model. We pray for people by grouping them into categories: the sick, the suffering, and so on. Notice that there is little mention of what we expect God to do for these people, except that we do ask (in one petition) for their salvation. Prayer is here not a list of commands for God: do this or that, for this or that person, but rather simply an act of bringing them before God, in love. It makes no sense to tell God about people as if He didn't know who they were or what they needed. That is partly why we only use first names in our prayers—God has known the name of each "from his mother's womb," and knows better for whom we are praying than we do ourselves.

Before my arrival at the university, there had been an old Russian bishop visiting Oxford, and he spent a great deal of time praying for people by name at the altar of preparation. Sometimes he was handed long lists of names written in Greek, which he found difficult both to read and to pronounce. The story goes that he used to lift such lists up in the air, so that God could read them for Himself.

If one examines the official prayers of the Church, there are comparatively few prayers where the person prays for himself. When this does occur, it is almost always to ask for forgiveness.

The wording of the Eleventh Step brings into focus an idea that resonates with the official prayer of the Church: The point of prayer is to learn what the will of God is. "Teach me to do Your will, for You are my God," and "in Your light we shall see light" (both from the Great Doxology).

Each member of the Body of Christ is enveloped in the love of God, a relationship that is forever growing, forever developing. When, in the Divine Liturgy, the Body of Christ (the worshippers) meets with and consumes the Body of Christ in the Chalice, the icon is perfected. For one moment, the identity of God and the identity of His children are no longer a matter of contrast, but of harmony. Ego-boundaries are fuzzy, and the Church inside the church participates in the life of God.

However, that moment only lasts forever at the end of time, when everything becomes real and the will of God is no longer experienced in hidden ways. Until then, we have to make do with a glimpse, a hint. But that hint gives us courage and hope. When we say farewell to the Body of Christ in the Chalice, we sing: "We have seen the true Light; we have received the heavenly Spirit; we have found the true Faith, worshipping the Undivided Trinity, who has saved us." Like the disciples leaving the scene of the Ascension of Our Lord, we return to our regular lives rejoicing in the fact that there, too, the will of God is as powerful and necessary as it is in the life-giving work of God Himself.

The practice of the priest at the time of the Prothesis is one that individuals may like to emulate in their own, private prayer. Compiling a list of people whom we encounter in the course of our lives, then praying for them on a regular basis ("Lord, remember . . .")

is a beautiful way of offering one's experience of life to God, and echoing at the same time the official prayer of the Church in the Divine Liturgy. Remembering family members, friends, teachers, and acquaintances is a powerful prayer, as we bring each name to God. After a while, the list becomes a sort of spiritual odyssey, reflecting the different stages of our lives, and the different people whom God has given us.

Of course, it is important to include people who have made negative contributions in our lives, as well as those who have contributed in a positive way. This allows us to fulfill the commandment to love our enemies in a simple and practical way. Reading the names of such people may bring us in touch with feelings we would prefer to ignore (or to get rid of altogether), but that is not the path that God places before us. We do not forgive our enemies by forgetting them. That is not forgiveness, that is forgetfulness. We forgive our enemies by praying for them. Even though our instincts and emotions go in quite other directions, that is what we are required to do.

For the Orthodox Christian, the word "meditation" may not immediately be useful, at least not at first sight, since it is not a word that is used a great deal in Orthodox literature. However, it is almost certain that the author of the Steps used the word to denote the quiet listening which is a necessary part of prayer, and which is very familiar in Orthodox practice.

In our own tradition, this "quietness" has been strongly amplified in the practice of the Jesus prayer. This short prayer, "Lord Jesus Christ, Son of God, have mercy," is suitable for beginners and for those approaching sanctity alike. It is a powerful weapon, a spiritual tool. Recited quietly, in the depth of our being, it becomes the heartbeat of prayer. Whether recited once or many times, slowly and purposefully, it quietens our mind and makes us available to God. It brings us toward the power of God to redeem and to save in a way that requires no imagination, no ego, no specialized knowledge: Lord, have mercy.

The use of the Jesus Prayer has become the most significant feature of the prayer life of many people. In the past it was considered the reserve of the extra-pious, and was rarely talked of outside monasteries. Of course, the prayer does not belong to any one person or group of persons—it is an element in the life of the Church. It is suitable for use by most people, and although it might be of great advantage to use it under the guidance of someone of spiritual stature, it is available to all, and may be used by all. Two five-minute periods of prayer during the course of the day may enliven one's prayer life in a dramatic way. However, it might not. We do not pray this prayer, or any other private prayer, *for* anything. We simply pray. The response is entirely the work of God, and that is completely beyond our control. All we have to do is make the effort.

There may be those for whom the Jesus Prayer is not satisfactory. In general, if someone is of a compulsive or obsessive nature, it might be better to find other, more active, forms of prayer. In this, as in so many other aspects of Church life, it is recommended that one consult a priest or someone recognized as having spiritual experience.

"Mercy" is a beautiful word, and focuses on the generosity of God. Freely given when not deserved, divine mercy is what makes it possible for us to become the children of God. It is a mistake, I think, to confuse "mercy" with "pity." "Pity," like "sympathy," is a word used for a series of feelings and actions that encourage people to hold onto their misery. "Oh, you poor thing" must be one of the most harmful sayings in the English language, since it inevitably invites the person addressed to stay in his or her pain in order to get more attention. "Mercy," on the other hand, serves as a universal healer, and encourages the individual to get on with life, not to stay stuck at an obstacle.

In Greek, the word has even more depth and significance. In the form with which we are most familiar (as in "Lord, have mercy," "*Kyrie eleison*") the word for "mercy" bears a striking resemblance to the word *elaion*, which means olive oil.

When I first went to Greece, from England, in the mid-seventies, I lived for a number of months at the Monastery of St. John the Evangelist on Patmos. I hardly spoke any Greek, and although I was warmly welcomed, I feel sure that most of the things that seemed important to me at the time must have mystified my hosts. I had so much to learn—how to live in a monastery, in a country far from home, in a language I did not know. I got to love the services, even in the middle of the night, although I had a definite preference for ordinary days, when the singing was brisk and with little interruption. For the major feast days, the monks invited one of the local priests on the island to come and sing. I am sure he had a good voice, but his style was wildly ornamental and operatic, and I found it difficult to endure. On those days the services were very long indeed, and not just because of their actual length.

Of all the things I recall, one of the most puzzling was the monthly ration of olive oil. At that time the monastery was run along the lines of an idiorhythmic house, that is, a monastery in which the monks had a degree of independence. In particular, each monk had to make his own arrangements when it came to food. He was given money and was expected to feed himself. In the normal course of events, what happened was that most of the monks got into little groups where they either took it in turns to cook, or they made some sort of arrangement for the cooking to be done. One monk, who had family living in the nearby town, received his food each day when the local bus arrived. His family owned a restaurant, and they prepared his food, wrapped it up, and sent it off.

I was assigned a deacon (I was a deacon, also, at this point) whose job it was to look after me, to cook for me, to keep me in order, and in general to show me the ropes. I think I must have made his life very difficult.

The most mystifying thing of all, however, and the point of this entire reminiscence, is that each monk in the monastery received a monthly allowance of olive oil. In England I had been used to having milk delivered to the house each day, but when I learned that we each had an olive oil allowance, and that it was brought round each month, I was more than a little baffled. What on earth could I find to do with something like a gallon of olive oil per month?

By the end of my time there, I found that I had often used my oil ration before the end of each month, and had to get more in the store. The oil was used for absolutely everything: cooking (for thickening, frying, and flavoring), and burning in the little lamps in front of the icons; it was used for cleaning certain items, and was the universal panacea for everything from a bad back to a swollen toe. It was the handyman's answer for what seemed like everything, and the general all-round support for daily life. That was what the olive oil was. It was healing and well-being in a bottle.

It is worth bearing in mind, then, that when we use the prayer "*Kyrie eleison*," we are (at least in the Greek parts of our imagination) also praying for olive oil, and for all the things it represents. Consider, too, that olive oil and the olive branch are the universal symbols for peace (poured on troubled waters and in the mouth of Noah's dove respectively), and so the prayer becomes a prayer for peace, as well.

Chapter 15

Spreading the Good News

Step 12: Having had a spiritual awakening as the result of these steps, we tried to carry this message to alcoholics, and to practice these principles in all our affairs.

Go home to your friends, and tell them what great things the Lord has done for you, and how He has had compassion on you. (Mark 5:19)

Let your light so shine before men, that they may see your good works and glorify your Father in heaven. (Matthew 5:16)

"I was hungry and you gave Me food; I was thirsty and you gave Me drink; I was a stranger and you took Me in; I was naked and you clothed Me; I was sick and you visited Me; I was in prison and you came to Me." Then the righteous will answer Him, saying, "Lord, when did we see You hungry and feed You, or thirsty and give You drink? When did we see You a stranger and take You in, or naked and clothe You? Or when did we see You sick, or in prison, and come to You?" And the King will answer and say to them, "Assuredly, I say to you, inasmuch as you did it to one of the least of these My brethren, you did it to Me." (Matthew 25:35–40)

Significance for an Addicted Person

Step Twelve is the realization of a life transformed. The person who started doing the Steps has become a different person. Here the riddle at the heart of the thinking and practice of AA makes most sense: Does the alcoholic become sober to do the Twelve Steps, or does he do the Twelve Steps to become sober?

It is possible, though extremely unlikely, that the person arriving at Step Twelve is still troubled, on a regular basis, by drinking.

181

Obviously, this is not because he cannot drink—he will always have the choice to go back to drinking—but because his new life has no place for drinking. He has looked at and come to terms with himself—good things and bad things; he has done what he could to repair areas in his life that needed repair. Most importantly, he has begun to mend his relationship with God, a process largely hidden in his heart, and deeply personal.

Even though personal, the nature of this new life, this "recovery," is something he cannot keep to himself. As with so much of life that is important—love, forgiveness, peace of mind—he can only keep what he gives away. If he tries to conserve it for himself, or worse, is afraid to share it for fear of losing it, he will lose it for sure.

Within the context of AA, where this Step has its original significance, this is a clear and real call for the alcoholic who has started to recover. There is no one who gets further than this—there is no such thing as a person who is "completely recovered." There is always more to learn, more to do, room for improvement. The relationship with God can always be deepened, or heightened. On the other hand, it is a contradiction in terms to talk about "partial recovery." Somewhere in the course of doing the work of the Steps the individual crosses a line. It is unlikely to be an earth-shattering conversion experience—which perhaps is strange, since that might be what one would expect. After all, the Steps have their roots deep within the American religious experience, a tradition which is often marked by the importance of a personal conversion experience, an awareness of being "reborn." One might also expect some version of the accompanying acceptance of God as one's personal Savior, common to the American evangelical experience. However, that is not present either. In the Steps, it is God who approaches the individual, not the individual who makes a conscious step toward God. Alcoholics are not very good at taking a conscious step in any direction!

Somewhere between starting the Steps and getting to Step Twelve, perhaps earlier, perhaps later, the alcoholic crosses a line, and his life is transformed. By the time he gets to the end of the Steps, he is ready to share his experience with others.

There have been times in the history of AA when the person who had twenty minutes of sobriety was able to guide the person who was still drinking. By the grace of God, that period has long passed, although in individual situations it may still be extremely important for particular individuals.

In the beginning, the first recovering alcoholics had a sense of what they needed to do in Step Twelve—they needed to carry the message to other alcoholics. Although it may seem odd, these people were actually motivated by selfish reasons. They felt sure that in order to keep their own sobriety, they had to pass it on. And that is what they did. At the very beginning, they would seek out drunks and try to convert them. That would be the obvious thing to do, given the background of the people involved. However, after a while it became clear that there were, in fact, two sorts of alcoholics in the world—those who were ready for recovery, because they had "hit bottom," and those who were not yet ready, those who had not "hit bottom." They found that trying to force recovery on people against their will was next to impossible. It was difficult enough trying to help those who wanted to get sober. However, those who wanted to recover were by far the better prospects. The ones who did not want to recover were more or less impossible.

As AA has grown older, the number of people getting better in AA has certainly grown, and it is also true that the majority of those who do recover find that AA is an indispensable part of their recovery—millions of people have achieved sobriety and recovery through belonging to AA. Naturally, as each new member achieves sobriety, the experience, the strength, and the hope of AA as a whole grows. The influence of AA grows as well. AA is busy spreading its message to alcoholics worldwide, including places that have been shut off to such influence in the past. Since AA has no allegiance to any particular religious doctrine, it is in a position to be of service under extremely diverse circumstances.

During the years, AA has had to adjust its thinking to allow for the fact that the medical profession, which has always had an interest in recovery from alcohol addiction, is now largely content to use the AA model of recovery in its treatment programs in hospitals and clinics. Judges and others in the world of law enforcement have seen the benefits of AA, and expect people to benefit by being forced to attend AA meetings.

The older pattern was that, once discovered, alcoholics would be visited, often at their home, by one or two AA members. This practice is called "Twelfth-Stepping" for obvious reasons. On knocking at the door, the visitors could never be certain what they were going to find. Sometimes what they found was a corpse—the call for help went out just too late. Sometimes they would find someone who had completely "forgotten" that he had called for help, and would be extremely resentful of the intrusion. They might find someone armed and dangerous—not uncommon, particularly in countries where weapons are readily available. The combination of alcohol and firearms is lethal under any circumstances. No amount of education will make a drunk person responsible for a gun.

Sometimes, though, the visitors would find someone who, though not necessarily very coherent, had obviously come to the conclusion that he (or she) had suffered enough, and though bewildered, was obviously ready to start out on the journey to recovery. Naturally, there may be many slips and slides on the way. Happy, indeed, is the person who gets sober through their first contact with AA. Nevertheless, once contact with AA has been made, the seeds of recovery are sown, even if they do not come to fruition for many years.

The conversation that occurs between the drinker and the AA members may be the first "real" conversation that person has had for a very long time. Sometimes the feelings of relief are immeasurable, and (depending on how much is remembered) the image of this meeting will last forever as a foundation for the new person's recovery. It may be the first important conversation for a long time that actually includes any kindness, or allows the alcoholic any feelings of dignity.

Although the people doing the Twelfth Step are entirely responsible for conducting the visit, they are not responsible for the outcome, nor do they take on the problems of the alcoholic.

Neither of these factors seems to make sense at first glance, but they contain very important information. As already stated, the AA members doing the Twelfth Step are doing so primarily for their own benefit. This is true both at an altruistic level (the basic need for human beings to help each other) and at a very practical level. By meeting with the drunk person, by seeing that person within the context of his own living arrangements (or lack of them), by encountering the dangers and the discomforts of active alcoholism, they are constantly reminded of their own past, and their own start in the Fellowship. They are always encouraged to compare their own experience with the experience of the person they are meeting, and to look for the ways in which it is similar, not the ways in which it is different. This is a basic theme in AA, and is true for each one of the Twelve Steps.

It is hardly a cliché to say that alcoholics most often die of terminal uniqueness. They feel that in the entire universe they are utterly unique, utterly alone. They like to believe that their own problems are not only greater than anyone else has ever had to face, but that they are also totally unsolvable. This is one of the ways in which they can support their destructive and difficult lifestyle. Once in the Fellowship, however, they find that their problems are, by and large, similar to the problems of nearly everyone else, particularly when they have learned the knack of looking for similarities (the new behavior) and giving little or no importance to the differences, which (until this point) had been their preferred outlook.

With the advent of treatment centers in almost every major hospital in the United States and elsewhere, the pattern of Twelfth-Stepping has changed a great deal. Waiting for an alcoholic to hit bottom has now been exchanged for attempting to bring the "bottom" up to hit the alcoholic, preferably hard, and on the chin (or indeed, any way that will get his attention, and will encourage him to leave his cocoon of denial and deceit). Naturally, treatment centers have to be profitable, in a way which AA does not have to be. AA takes quite serious steps to make sure it is never motivated by the bottom line, or any other manifestation of money or prestige.

AA has no shareholders, is self-supporting through its own contributions, and regards almost all but the most necessary contacts with money as an "outside interest"—i.e. a topic which diverts from the primary purpose, which is to help alcoholics who are still suffering. Much of this policy comes from the early experience of the Fellowship, when most of the temptations of alcoholics, in particular grandiosity, were encountered with full force and soundly rejected.

This is not to say that individual AA members are not involved in treatment centers. On the contrary, if these centers are going to use the AA program in some form or other, it is perhaps just as well that they employ people who have a good working knowledge of the Steps. However, this situation does not actually affect AA as a whole. There are AA members in almost all walks of life, and it would be very strange if they were not free to work in treatment centers, if that is where their abilities lie.

This does not mean, however, that treatment centers take the place of the local meetings of AA. Nor does it mean that the treatment centers cannot have their own AA meetings. Under most circumstances, any group of people wishing to call themselves a group of Alcoholics Anonymous is able to do so.

The sad thing is that meetings in treatment centers are not always the powerhouses of sobriety that are found elsewhere. Most group meetings benefit from having a wide variety of membership—from different walks of life, different social backgrounds and ages. In a treatment center, the one thing that binds most people together is not the desire to stop drinking, but the necessity of being in a treatment center, whether voluntarily or not. For this reason, it is always a good idea for such centers to encourage AA members in the district to attend these meetings, as their presence can often make such a meeting much more productive.

AA does not try to force anyone to do anything. Treatment centers aim at achieving a goal (usually immediate sobriety, with aftercare which probably involves attendance at AA meetings). While AA is bound to assist and cooperate with treatment centers at a certain level (since they house alcoholics who want to stop drinking), AA needs to remain separate and distinct in its government and organization in order to be true to the Traditions by which it governs its activities. In many respects these Traditions (twelve in number, just like the Steps) are as important as the Steps because they place the working of the Steps within a safe, spiritual environment.

Ultimately, for the alcoholic who finds sobriety, the main prize is the "spiritual awakening" that is the result of doing the Steps. Carrying the message to others is simply an expression of that awakening.

For the Orthodox Christian

On the Sunday of Orthodoxy, the First Sunday of Great Lent, we read the story of Philip and Nathanael. In it we find the following lines:

> Philip found Nathanael and said to him, "We have found him of whom Moses in the law, and also the prophets, wrote—Jesus of Nazareth, the son of Joseph." And Nathanael said to him, "Can anything good come out of Nazareth?" Philip said to him, "Come and see" (John 1:45, 46).

Here, in a very distinct and succinct manner, is the model by means of which the Orthodox Church has spread during much of the last two thousand years: "Come and see!"

In general, the aggressive methods of proselytism favored by many Protestant groups (and, in some respects, by the Roman Catholic Church as well) have not been the normal behavior of Orthodox Christians. Indeed, for much of the two thousand years of history, the notion of individual conversion from one religion to another would have been unthinkable. Families, yes, tribes, perhaps, nations, certainly. But the notion of individual conversion, though now the normative image, has to be regarded as something of a modern invention, and one which does not fit with the whole picture of the history of the Orthodox Church very well.

The Orthodox Church possesses an awareness that she is the

true Church of Christ, and that only within the Orthodox Church can be found the fullness of the Christian Faith. However, when she makes this claim, it is with a sense of deepest humility and in deepest gratitude. Through all the twists and turns of Church history, particularly in the periods when the doctrine of the Church was being developed, great efforts were made, sometimes at enormous personal cost, to get as close as possible to the truth. This process, however, was not speculative, nor was it seen in terms of numerical or political success. Orthodoxy was not to be invented, but discovered, and the process of that discovery took many strange twists. Often the champions of Orthodoxy were seen as failures during their lifetimes, and on a number of occasions, those who upheld Orthodox doctrine were a small minority among the majority of believers. On three occasions in particular, Orthodoxy has been defended by lone figures—St. Athanasios in the fourth century, St. Maximos the Confessor in the seventh, and St. Mark of Ephesus in the fifteenth century.

The criterion for Orthodoxy, then, is not that it is something good or perfect in men's eyes, but rather that it is something good in God's eyes. That is what makes Orthodoxy what its name implies—"right-glory," an authentic expression of the worshipping Church.

This situation, then, runs counter to notions that the Orthodox Church has to be the biggest, or the best, or the most powerful. Indeed, she does not need to claim such attributes, since she, as a whole, is the expression of the truth of God.

If, then, the Orthodox Church possesses the truth of God, the fullness of the Christian revelation, then ultimately the success or otherwise of the Church is in God's care, not ours. It is our task to be the best that we can be, but it is not our task to try to convince others of the rightness of our cause.

When I was growing up, I met an old priest. He was remarkable in many ways, not least because I think he was the first alcoholic I ever met. The only part of his alcoholism I recognized was the fact that he would often drink before the service, always after the service, and sometimes even during the service. Since altar wine is almost always available in the altar, it was perhaps inevitable that he should do so. As far as I recall, he died without ever coming to terms with his drinking.

More remarkable still, perhaps, was his spiritual astuteness, and the depth of his spiritual vision. It was as if God overlooked his most glaring character defect, and still allowed him to glimpse the heights of heaven. He was a kindly man, and he used to like to say a special prayer with the altar boys before dismissing them at the end of the Liturgy. I cannot remember the whole prayer, but it contained a line something like this: "When we leave this place, may we live in a way that lets the world know that we have been with Jesus." By this, he did not mean pious frowning, or a look of religion. He meant that by our demeanor, by everything about us, it should be obvious that we had been in the presence of Jesus, as if people driving past the church would point and stare at us as we emerged.

This notion, difficult though it might be, fits in very well with AA's idea about spreading the message of AA. It is to be done through attraction rather than promotion. As Orthodox we should live our lives in such a way that our religious lives should become irresistible to others with whom we share the world. At no point in the Gospel does Christ ask us to be right. He asks us to repent. He asks us to be good.

The presence of an Orthodox community in an area should be felt in terms of the love and service that emanate from it. A self-serving Orthodox community does nothing to further the Kingdom, except perhaps, in making the light of Orthodoxy available to successive generations; even then it is a pale and sad vision of Orthodoxy that is handed on.

The presence of Orthodox churches and chapels should be very real expressions of the presence of God in our society. In Greece, the landscape is scattered with chapels, many of them tiny, most of them used just once a year. However, they are a strong expression of the presence of God on that landscape. They are truly points of light, because each represents the Kingdom made manifest within human society.

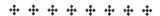

HERE IS ONE DESCRIPTION THAT COULD BE APPLIED to someone who has worked through the Twelve Steps and goes on to use his experience to enliven his awareness of God:

> A man who stands on a high place breathing fresh air is filled with more cheerfulness and strength than someone who stands below in darkness breathing gloomy, stagnant air. Likewise the man who, because of his hope on the promises of the Spirit, labors with steadfast faith, receives greater consolation, joy, encouragement, and is more sanctified by the Spirit, than the man who with remorse, sorrow, bitterness and distress of heart labors in self-applied compulsion without the consolation of reaching the harbor of hope. (St. Isaac the Syrian)[14]

---

14 From the *Ascetical Homilies*, App. b, 1:50, p. 398, Holy Transfiguration Monastery, Boston MA, 1984.

Chapter 16

Slogans and Sayings

HERE ARE A FEW OF THE SLOGANS AND SAYINGS, official and unofficial, that can be heard in and around Twelve Step meetings and that help people to stay focused on their recovery. They are universally acknowledged to be trite, even if they are not actually clichés. However, if they keep just one person alive, they may be forgiven their naïveté.

1   Take the cotton wool out of your ears and stuff it in your mouth.

Although this is not the most polite of the sayings commonly heard at meetings of Twelve Step Fellowships, nevertheless it contains a great deal of wisdom.

No one will be very surprised to learn that drinking alcoholics are bad listeners. In fact, they usually live in an environment where almost no listening takes place. In the normal alcoholic household, there is a lot of talking but almost no listening. Communication is a difficult area for all human beings, and alcoholics and their families are particularly bad at it. What conversations do take place tend to be copies of ones that have taken place many times before. It is more like a script than an effort to exchange information.

The average mind is full of presuppositions at best, prejudices at worst. The addict has the same condition, but in much greater measure. The ability to listen with an open mind, or perhaps more precisely with an open heart, is a necessary prerequisite to recovery.

It is the practice of monasteries to impose silence on people who are just starting out on their monastic path. Whether it is a silence of a few hours or for a lengthy period of time, the message is the same: it is better to listen than to speak. Speaking gets a lot of young people into trouble, and young monks and nuns are no exception. Spending some time in the knowledge that one does not have to offer an opinion, defend an opinion, or otherwise make a remark in his new family has the effect of relieving one from the need to dominate, or the need to gain attention.

Listening is the beginning of obedience, and that is true whether we are listening to God or to another human being. Although the sort of obedience demanded in monasteries is seldom asked for outside the monastic family (indeed, it is hardly safe to do so), it is good to remember that listening, not speaking, is the beginning of spiritual growth.

In regards to prayer, it is possible to interpret Step Eleven, which encourages prayer and meditation, as referring to prayer that is spoken, and prayer that is listening. Reading Sacred Scripture in a slow and meditative manner, an activity that has an important place in the life of the Church, is also listening.

When people join Twelve Step Fellowships, the most important ability they need to develop is that of listening, because most of what they need to know in order to start recovering from their condition is going to be gained through their ears. At the other end of the spectrum, the saint is constantly listening to God. In between, there is a great deal of listening to do.

2 Let go and let God.

This simple-sounding recipe has at its heart the ultimate expression of a sound spiritual relationship between God and man. So long as a person is fighting to control his own life, he is precluding the action of God within that life. As soon as he lets go—as soon as he surrenders—he starts to win.

The following poem, originally in Dutch, was written by someone during the first days of his recovery:

Just For Today

We must surrender to win the fight
We die in order to live
We go through sickness to gain our health
We have to give away what we want to keep
Herein lies the paradox of surrender.

3 One day at a time

Life is met one day at a time, one moment at a time. Addicts are good at trying to solve the problems of the entire universe and trying to make history bend to their own needs. In recovery, one of the most important factors to learn is that one need only face up to the problems of one day at a time. Jesus expressed this in the words, "Do not worry about tomorrow, for tomorrow will worry about its own things. Sufficient for the day *is* its own trouble" (Matthew 6:34).

4 Easy does it . . .

Alcoholics try to storm their way into heaven, picking up even the nuance of a difficulty and turning it into a war. Very often it is necessary for them (and for others too) to stop trying so hard. Essentially, God is in charge, and although we may not like to acknowledge it, He was running the universe pretty well before we came on the scene, and will presumably continue to do so long after we have gone. Seeing oneself with the right perspective is very important.

5 First things first

Alcoholics want to do everything all at once, and generally cannot see the difference between things that matter and things that do not. They are absolutely hopeless when it comes to making priorities. They live in an "all or nothing" world in which they regularly end up with their second choice. It is crucial for them to see that things need to be kept simple, and that the most important things are the ones remembered first. For the alcoholic, this involves remembering that the whole point of sobriety is to be able to live without drinking alcohol. If this is not set as a priority, the chances are he will drink once more.

6 Live and let live.

The whole attitude of the Steps to personal progress, whether essentially spiritual in nature or even in some other aspect of life, is that one is capable of making decisions for oneself, but one is not capable of making decisions for anyone else. Remember, the alcoholic originally wants to solve all his problems by changing the rest of the world. In sobriety he quickly learns that he has to keep a close eye on his own thoughts, actions, and beliefs, but that he does not have to be the watchdog for everyone else. He learns to put all his religious strengths, for example, into transforming his own life, not trying to change other people. This situation does not mysteriously change at some point in his recovery, even if he is a politician.

7   But for the grace of God . . .

It sometimes happens that recovering alcoholics meet drinking alcoholics. When that occurs, the recovering alcoholic is supposed to bear this slogan in mind. The idea is not that he should get some sort of smug feeling of superiority—on the contrary—at this point he should be acutely aware that his first reaction should be one of gratitude, since but for the grace of God he would be in exactly the same condition as the drunk person. This saying can be adapted for any situation in which gratitude is required.

8   Keep it simple.

Alcoholics hate simplicity, because they cannot control it. They prefer complexity, preferably to the point where no one else can understand what they are talking about. Then the alcoholic is in complete control. However, he is also in a minority of one, and his position is both needless and harmful.

Sometimes this saying is lengthened to read, "Keep it simple, stupid," which gives the acronym KISS. This is a customary self-criticism of a person's own actions whenever he has dealt with something in a convoluted or pompous manner.

Another important acronym is HALT—short for "hungry, angry, lonely, and tired," the four conditions in which it is necessary for a recovering alcoholic to consider calling another recovering person before picking up a drink.

9   Gratitude

Gratitude is the most basic of human reactions to God. Many people use it to focus themselves, because an expression of gratitude puts one into a fairly immediate state of relationship with God. Giving thanks is very basic, yet is also involved in the highest sense of giving offerings to God—particularly in the Divine Liturgy. An uttered "thank you," even said through clenched teeth, is often sufficient to bring a person into a spiritual frame of mind.

10 There is no defense against the first drink.

The alcoholic is taught that he does not have to fear the sixth drink or the tenth—the ones he has always (until now) claimed have ruined his life. It is quite categorically the first drink that is fatal to him—the drink that is taken in (relative) sobriety. He does not have to fear committing a felony while he is in an alcoholic blackout; he does not have to fear being incarcerated in an institution for the criminally insane; he does not have to fear losing his job, his family, or his freedom—he just has to learn to fear the first drink. It is representational of the whole drinking process, from placing the glass to the lips to placing the casket in the ground. So long as he does not take the first drink, he cannot get drunk, and the tenth drink becomes irrelevant.

Furthermore, the recovering alcoholic can rest peacefully in the knowledge that he has no power, of his own being, to avoid drinking again. The power to stop him drinking belongs to God alone, and it is in cooperation with the will of God that the alcoholic will make sobriety a reality in his own life.

11 I may have another drunk in me, but I do not have another recovery.

This is an often-heard saying, particularly among older people. Every alcoholic can get drunk again. Each alcoholic is only one drink away from a drunk—these are certainties. What is not certain, however, is that having got drunk again, a person could find his way back to sobriety. For a number of reasons, it is not worth experimenting with, and a saying like this is used to underline that fact.

12 Acceptance

Acceptance is the opposite of denial. Just as denial implies the inability or lack of desire to accept the way God has organized the universe, so acceptance is an attitude of trust that allows God to be God, even when we do not like or do not understand the details

God presents to us. It is sometimes helpful to accept the fact that the details we can see form part of a bigger picture that we cannot see. It is entirely acceptable to believe that God has a plan for every level of existence, but that we, as individuals, may never actually know what that plan is—at least, not in this lifetime. The ability to predict the mind of God is not acceptance. The ability to take what God gives without inner turmoil is at the heart of the experience of acceptance, as this story indicates:

There was once a poor farmer who had one son and a small field somewhere in the mountains of Greece during the period of Turkish rule. Life was hard and life was short.

One day, as the poor farmer was working in his field, a beautiful white horse appeared and stood near the farmer, grazing quietly on the grass.

As news of this fact became known, the farmer's neighbors all came round, congratulating him on his find. "Aren't you lucky!" they said. "Now you will be able to use the horse to plow the field and pull the cart to market, and you will become a rich man."

The old man smiled gently. "I do not know whether I am lucky or not," he replied. "All I know is, I was working in my field, when suddenly this horse came and started grazing. *Etsi einai*[15]—that's just what happened."

On the following days the horse stayed, but no one came to collect the animal, so the farmer's son decided to see if he could ride him. Although the boy had no saddle, he found that the horse was quite content to let him sit on his back, and away they went. Unfortunately, after a while, they came to a low-lying branch, and the farmer's son was knocked from the horse, fell to the ground, and broke his leg.

The farmer's neighbors came running. "How unlucky you are," they said. "Your son has fallen off the horse and broken his leg. He won't be able to help you in the field, and you will most likely starve."

The old man smiled gently. "As to whether I am lucky or

---

15 A standard Greek expression, roughly translated (with a shrug of the shoulders) "that's just how it is."

unlucky I cannot say," he replied. "All I know is that I was working in my field, and the beautiful white horse appeared; my son tried to ride him, but fell off, breaking his leg. *Etsi einai*—that is just what happened."

Two days later, a troop of the Sultan's guard arrived in the village, looking for recruits for the army. At that time the Sultan was waging a battle against a powerful enemy. The soldiers found the farmer's son (who would have been an ideal soldier), but when they realized that the boy had a broken leg, they left him and went on to the next village, to find recruits there.

When they heard the news, the villagers came running. "How lucky you are," they said. "The Sultan's men came to take away your son, but when they realized that he had a broken leg, they left him and went on to the next village. God must really love you."

The old man smiled gently. "As to whether I am lucky or unlucky I cannot say," he replied. "All I know is that I was working in my field, and a beautiful white horse appeared; my son tried to ride him, but fell off, and broke his leg. The Sultan's guard came to take my son away to the army, but when they found him with a broken leg, they left him and went off to the next village. *Etsi einai*—that is just what happened."

Days passed, and the boy's leg started to heal. However, one morning the farmer woke up and found that the horse had disappeared during the night.

When they heard the news, the villagers came running. "How unlucky you are," they said. "The beautiful white horse has gone—such a fine animal, and valuable too. What a terrible loss. You have nothing left to live for."

The old man smiled gently. "As to whether I am lucky or unlucky I cannot say," he replied. "All I know is that I was working in my field, and a beautiful white horse appeared; my son tried to ride him, but fell off and broke his leg. The Sultan's guard came to take my son away to the army, but when they found him with a broken leg, they left him and went off to the next village. Then the beautiful horse disappeared in the middle of the night. *Etsi einai*—that is just what happened."

As the days passed, the farmer's son's health improved, and eventually he was able to walk again. When he was well enough, he decided that he would go to look for the beautiful white horse.

Days went by, and the farmer continued to work in his fields. Sometimes it was hot, and sometimes it was cold, and occasionally it was just right.

Several months later, the farmer's son returned. "You'll never guess what happened," he said. "I followed the tracks of the horse as best I could, and eventually caught up with him about twenty miles away. On his back was riding the most beautiful girl I have ever seen. Eventually I asked her father for her hand in marriage, and as a dowry he gave me the white horse. So now I have returned, the horse has returned, and I have the most beautiful wife in the world."

As news of this went round, the neighbors came rushing in. "How fortunate you are!" they all said. "Your son went off to look for your horse, and returned not only with the horse, but also with a beautiful new bride. How lucky you are! You must be the luckiest man alive."

The old man smiled gently. "Whether I am lucky or not I cannot say. All I know is that I was working in the field and the horse appeared. My son rode the horse and fell off, breaking his leg. The Sultan's soldiers came to take my son away, but once they saw he had a broken leg, they left him here. The horse ran away, and when my son found him, he also found the wife of his dreams, and brought her back here. *Etsi einai*—that is just what happened."

Months passed, and one day the old man died.

When news got round, the neighbors all came running. "How sad this is!" they said to the young man. "Just when everything was going so well, your father died." The young man said nothing, but showed the neighbors into the room where his father lay.

There was a faint smile on the old man's lips.

Chapter 17

After the Steps?

THE TWELVE STEPS ARE A CHALLENGE in the same way that the Gospel is a challenge. One may choose to ignore the challenge, yet still lead a seemingly satisfactory life. However, both the Gospel and the Steps offer the gift of transformation for those who seek.

Under most circumstances, it is possible for Christians to avoid the more difficult challenges of the Gospel. This they do because to answer the Gospel will often mean a radical adjustment of their own lives, and a reevaluation of subjects like prejudice, economics, honesty, humility, personal power, and personal possessions. We Christians—all of us, of all persuasions—exert a great deal of effort in making sure that we manage to avoid some of the big issues, and we do this in a number of different ways.

One of the most popular methods of avoiding the Gospel is to confuse thinking about its teachings with actually carrying those teachings out. For example, we might hear in the Gospel that we are obliged to love our enemies, and for a while, standing in church, we may even contemplate what it would mean to do just that. Unfortunately, as often as not, as we leave church we may be tempted to consider that by simply contemplating loving our enemies, we have actually fulfilled the command of Christ; we then go about our business, perhaps with a little more self-satisfaction than before. Unfortunately, thinking about the subject, even seriously, is not what is called for. Our Lord Himself (and all the saints of every age) calls for action.

The commandment to refrain from judging others seems a good idea within the context of the Sermon on the Mount, and we may actually savor its meaning and its implications. However, in reality we know that we find it thoroughly impractical in day-to-day living; few people would use it as a rule in the boardroom, for example, or in a court of law.

The fact that the Gospel contains some difficult demands does not give us permission to ignore its sayings. Even though the Gospels contain some very difficult, challenging texts, full of subtleties, they nevertheless contain sublime truth. Certainly they are complex pieces of spiritual writing, whose significance is most fully experienced within the Church for whom its words were written. However, they should be read and reread until their words live in our awareness. Just picking up one of the Gospels and reading it is rarely enough to effect a change in a person's life, at least in the modern world.

The society in which Jesus lived was very different from our own. He grew up in a country ruled by the brutal occupying force of a foreign empire. This must have left a deep impression on Him, and it is not difficult to see how He adapted some of His teaching to contemporary issues. "If a man compels you to go one mile" was not a hypothetical issue—it was a daily occurrence, since Roman soldiers were entitled to demand just that sort of service from the local inhabitants. Even so, knowing that His teaching would be most unpopular, Jesus required that a person in that situation offer to go two miles. Loving enemies was no easier two thousand years ago than it is today.

There have been many changes since the time of Jesus. Empires and entire religious systems have come and gone since then; political and economic conditions have brought entirely different sets of challenges to the modern world. It is possible that the whole theme of addiction and addictive behavior exists in today's world in a way it did not two thousand years ago. Even though St. Paul may be hinting at addiction (or addictive behavior) when he says: "For the good that I will *to do,* I do not do; but the evil I will not *to do,* that I practice" (Romans 7:19), he may simply be talking more generally about the human propensity for doing wrong.

However, it is worth bearing in mind that addiction is a force in the modern world, even if it was not two thousand years ago. Fueled by affluence, together with a growing lack of purpose and identity, addiction is probably a more important problem for more people in the modern world than it ever was for any but a small fraction of our ancestors.

Just as it is now standard for blood to be tested for HIV anti-bodies before being given to patients in transfusions, so it may be necessary for more and more people and even groups of people to be tested for addiction, and for the many variations of addiction, before they can use other forms of personal, or spiritual, development.

If indeed addiction is a modern problem, the Steps are a modern solution. Nevertheless, addiction will never replace sin as the ultimate challenge to God, and the Steps will never replace the Gospels as the call of Christ.

At the end of the nineteenth century, St. Theophan the Recluse wrote:

If the main goal of the repentant sinner should be total, light-bearing and blessed communion with God, then the main hindrance to this is the existence of the passions still active and working in him—the virtues being as yet unsealed in him—and the unrighteousness of his powers. Therefore his main work on conversion and repentance should be the uprooting of passions and sealing the virtues—in a word, correcting himself. (Bishop Theophan the Recluse: *The Path to Salvation*)

The main difficulty in applying the words of St. Theophan in today's world is that the human will (i.e. the part that "corrects himself") is, in his example, totally dedicated to God. Unfortunately, in our understanding of the alcoholic or any other addict, this is simply not the case. The part of the human personality that he needs to use to correct himself is diseased to the point that it cannot make the necessary decisions; it cannot, since it is entirely lacking in integrity.

In Step 26 of the *Ladder of Divine Ascent,* the author makes the following comment: "He who wishes to present his body pure to Christ, and to show Him a clean heart, must carefully preserve chastity and freedom from anger, for without these our labor is quite useless." On hearing these words, an addict has no idea where to begin. The spiritual tools mentioned as being required are so far from his grasp that he cannot even imagine what a life of chastity and freedom from anger might be like.

Telling an addict to "do better," "try harder," or anything of the sort is completely useless. He needs to be treated for his addiction first, before this sort of advice makes any sense to him.

It is precisely this sort of treatment that the Steps are able to provide. The Steps are written for everyman. They are unsophisticated, blunt, and allow almost no room for personal interpretation. They are so direct in their language, so uncompromising in their wording, that there is absolutely no doubt about what they mean, at least in the areas that matter. The Steps do not attempt to contain divine truth, nor do they reveal anything eternal. They simply suggest to people what to do if they want to get better from alcoholism, and are used more generally by people recovering from all sorts of addictions.

They might as easily be used to lead the sinner to repentance.

Though the Steps may be used with great benefit for the development of a spiritual life, they, of themselves, claim no saving grace. For the alcoholic, all the Steps do is present the possibility of sober living. That life starts where the Twelve Steps finish. However, the Steps do not even guarantee that an alcoholic person who has done all twelve of them will necessarily be able to remain abstinent from alcohol for the rest of his life. Sobriety requires effort, and more than anything else, willingness.

The Steps call us to a path of integrity in which it is more difficult to avoid the commands of the Gospel. The Steps call for rigorous honesty, fearless self-evaluation, the explicit righting of wrongs, and a vision of human existence in which it is God who rules the universe, not one's own ego, or that of someone else. The Steps pull the committed Christian toward the Gospel. In so many ways, the Steps are not the end, but a means. Just as there is no sense in which one can complete the Steps fully, so it is also true that they have no sense of completion within themselves—they lead on to greater things.

The idea that one can "graduate" after doing the Twelve Steps is misleading. Although they constitute, in some senses, a straight line which needs to be started at the beginning and continued, in order, until they are finished, the wording of the Steps themselves reveals that this is not the whole picture. At one level, for example, the wording of Steps Ten and Eleven refers to the continuation of processes started in earlier steps. Step Twelve refers to the state of "spiritual awakening" that is gained as the result of doing the previous eleven Steps. The Steps form a spiral, but like a spiritual Mobius strip, it turns out that the step following Step Twelve is Step One—not where it was the last time it was encountered, but now matching the needs and the problems of the "new" person who has been born while working the Steps.

Over the course of time, naturally, it turns out that once one has done the Twelve Steps in order to look at a single and pressing problem (usually the one causing the most pain), there are other problems that need to be looked at. On a practical level, it might be that someone has managed to start learning a great deal about sobriety from alcohol, but now that person realizes his use of cigarettes is not good, or that he is overweight, or that he has a tortuous relationship with money, or that his business practices are a little too sharp.

Having done the Twelve Steps, the person may have encountered a new level of understanding about what it means to be a good person, and this understanding inevitably calls for change. It is the journey, not the destination, that is important.

Does this mean that by starting the Twelve Steps, a person is condemning himself to seeking ways to improve his life for the rest of eternity? In a sense, yes. Neither completion nor complacency is the essence of any of the Twelve Steps; it is progress, not perfection, that is valued. With God's help, the good can become better, the not-so-good can be improved.

This will always be true.

Appendix A

The Twelve Steps for General Use

1. We admitted we were powerless (over _____)—that our lives had become unmanageable.
2. Came to believe that a Power greater than ourselves could restore us to sanity.
3. Made a decision to turn our will and our lives over to the care of God *as we understood Him.*
4. Made a searching and fearless moral inventory of ourselves.
5. Admitted to God, to ourselves, and to another human being the exact nature of our wrongs.
6. Were entirely ready to have God remove all these defects of character.
7. Humbly asked Him to remove our shortcomings.
8. Made a list of all the persons we had harmed and became willing to make amends to them all.
9. Made direct amends to such people wherever possible, except when to do so would injure them or others.
10. Continued to take personal inventory and when we were wrong promptly admitted it.
11. Sought through prayer and meditation to improve our conscious contact with God *as we understood Him,* praying only for knowledge of His will for us and the power to carry that out.
12. Having had a spiritual awakening as the result of these steps, we tried to carry this message to others and to practice these principles in all our affairs.

Appendix B

The Twelve Traditions
of Alcoholics Anonymous

1. Our common welfare should come first; personal recovery depends on AA unity.
2. For our group purpose there is but one ultimate authority—a loving God as He may express Himself in our group conscience. Our leaders are but trusted servants; they do not govern.
3. The only requirement for AA membership is a desire to stop drinking.
4. Each group should be autonomous except in matters affecting other groups or AA as a whole.
5. Each group has but one primary purpose—to carry its message to the alcoholic who still suffers.
6. An AA group ought never endorse, finance or lend the AA name to any related facility or outside enterprise, lest problems of money, property and prestige divert us from our primary purpose.
7. Every AA group ought to be fully self-supporting, declining outside contributions.
8. Alcoholics Anonymous should remain forever nonprofessional, but our service centers may employ special workers.
9. AA, as such, ought never be organized; but we may create service boards or committees directly responsible to those they serve.
10. Alcoholics Anonymous has no opinion on outside issues; hence the AA name ought never be drawn into public controversy.
11. Our public relations policy is based on attraction rather than promotion; we need always maintain personal anonymity at the level of press, radio and film.
12. Anonymity is the spiritual foundation of all our traditions, ever reminding us to place principles before personalities.

About the Author

Archimandrite Meletios Webber was received into the Orthodox Church by Bishop Kallistos Ware in 1971. He was educated at Dulwich College and Oxford University, and has a doctorate in psychological counseling. Fr. Meletios has served the Orthodox Church in Greece, Great Britain, the US, and the Netherlands, and is currently living in the Netherlands. He is also the author of *Bread & Water, Wine & Oil: An Orthodox Christian Experience of God* (Ancient Faith, 2007).

Visit our Ancient Faith Publishing website at store.ancientfaith.com

We hope you have enjoyed and benefited from this book. Your financial support makes it possible to continue our nonprofit ministry both in print and online. Because the proceeds from our book sales only partially cover the costs of operating **Ancient Faith Publishing** and **Ancient Faith Radio**, we greatly appreciate the generosity of our readers and listeners. Donations are tax-deductible and can be made at **www.ancientfaith.com.**

To view our other publications,
please visit our website: **store.ancientfaith.com**

Bringing you Orthodox Christian music, readings,
prayers, teaching, and podcasts 24 hours a day since 2004 at
www.ancientfaith.com